Nick Page is an author and broadcaster whose books include *The Tabloid Bible*, *Keep It Simple*, *The Tabloid Shakespeare* and *The Dead Sea Files*.

As the author of a novel featuring a man with two noses and a talking gerbil, some might say that he deserves to be featured in this book, but he is keen to point out that 'it is not as bad as it sounds'.

He lives in Oxfordshire with his wife, three children and a Morris Minor called Ken. He supports Watford Football Club, but then again, so do a lot of people, I mean, it's not necessarily a sign of mental imbalance…

He is currently at work on the biography of a seventeenth-century dwarf. No, really.

More information at www.nickpage.co.uk

In Search of the World's Worst Writers

A Celebration of Triumphantly Bad Literature

Nick Page

HarperCollins*Publishers*

HarperCollins*Publishers*
77–85 Fulham Palace Road, London W6 8JB
www.fireandwater.com

First published in Great Britain in 2000
by HarperCollins*Publishers*

1 3 5 7 9 10 8 6 4 2

Every effort has been made to trace the ownership of
copyright items in this collection and to obtain permission
for their use. The publisher would appreciate notification of,
and copyright details for, any instances where further
acknowledgement is due.

A catalogue record for this book is available
from the British Library.

ISBN 0 00 274094 X

Printed and bound in Great Britain
by Omnia Books Ltd, Glasgow

Oh you critics! – if an author errs in a single line
That line you'll surely quote,
And will give it as a sample fair
Of all he ever wrote.
J. Gordon Coogler, 'You Critics'

He chopped and changed his original article in such a way that it was
something quite beyond the most bewildering article he had written
in the past; and is still prized by those highly cultured persons who
collect the worst literature in the world.
G.K. Chesterton, *The Flying Inn*

Contents

Introduction

In 1838 a librarian compiled a list of what the public were borrowing from his library. We are told that during that year, 166 people borrowed 'Novels by Walter Scott', 439 people took 'Fashionable novels, well known' and a disappointing 27 people borrowed 'Works of a good character'. 1008 readers borrowed what the compiler termed 'Fashionable Novels, containing no good, although probably nothing decidedly bad'. And, right at the bottom of the list comes the following entry:

Books decidedly bad   10

I don't know what the books were that those ten readers borrowed, but I like to think that some of the writers in this volume were among them. And I am certain that, had I wandered into that library, I too would have ignored the 'fashionable novels' and the 'works of a good character' and headed straight for the section labelled 'decidedly bad'.

For years I have been scouring bookshops, libraries, magazines and junk stores for the world's worst writers – that select band of literary pioneers whose writing is so bad they have arrived at genius from the wrong direction.

It all started with my father-in-law. Derek was a man with many talents, but poetry was not one of them, as his family discovered one day when he showed us a poem he had written when he was young. The poem, called 'On Coronation Day', celebrated the coronation of King George VI and included the memorable lines:

The King will hold the Orb of Gold
The Sceptre he shall take

Also the crown that's very old
It took some time to make.[1]

Derek was always a generous soul and didn't seem to resent the fact that his family, far from being awe-struck by the majestic pomp of his verse actually spent the next few hours crying with laughter.[2] But from that moment I was hooked. Let others deal with the towering heights of literature – I was heading in the opposite direction.

This is the result of my labours. Apart from a handful of the most well-known exponents, their work has long been out of print, only available tucked away on the shelves of secondhand book shops or in libraries where the works are usually locked in a secure cupboard for the public's safety.

At times, I must admit, the search was hard going. It has meant many hours trudging through barren wastelands of tedious drivel. But it was worth it, for just when I thought there were no new delights to be found and nothing truly awful left to discover, I would unearth a gem, a jewel of breath-taking dreadfulness. It was like discovering a diamond on a slagheap.

Such gems can be found in all genres and across all nationalities. Although most of the writers in this book are poets, the reader will also find extracts from extraordinarily bad novels, travel guides, philosophical speculations and even a wonderfully abysmal Portuguese-English dictionary. Of the 42 featured writers, 26 are British, 12 are American, and there are one each from Canada, France, Portugal and Russia. They come from all walks of life – everyone from duchesses to

---

[1] Well, no-one ever thought it was knocked up in a day.

[2] This poem is packed with goodies. Another favourite verse runs:

This day shall ne'er be forgot
For at least a hundred years
And all the people that are old
Will hear it in their ears.

Alas, he never continued with his poetry. Tragic – he could have been one of the all-time greats.

potato salesmen; from chicken farmers to millionaires. The only thing they have in common is their devotion to their work, and their utter inability to write.

Naturally this is a personal selection. These are the writers I consider the worst, the curdled *crème de la crème*. You may have your own favourites. Indeed, I hope that the publication of this book will lead to many more discoveries from my readers. There are, after all, many crowns still left to be claimed. The worst technical manual is still awaiting discovery and the number of playwrights in this collection is surely not representative of the amount of awful dramas that have been produced since the time of Shakespeare. I am particularly keen to find the worst journalist ever, although the field must be incredibly vast.

I have also, deliberately, not chosen any writer still alive, partly from the fear of offending anyone, partly because I doubt they would allow me permission to include them in a book of the 'worst writers' anyway, but mainly for fear that I myself would suddenly become eligible.

Although I have no doubt that all of the selected writers would have been absolutely mortified to find themselves included in this book, it is meant as a tribute. I would not want anyone to think that I look down on any of these writers – on the contrary, I admire them intensely. Often their lot in life was hard. Convinced of their own greatness, they trod a lonely path, stubborn in their belief that their work was worthwhile, even though virtually everyone else fell about laughing. None of these writers deserve to be forgotten. In their own warped way, they have all contributed something unique to the history of literature.

So, if it seems that I am merely adding to the abuse and ridicule that they have suffered, then I can only say in my defence that I love these writers and admire them greatly.

No, really.

Nick Page
Oxfordshire, March 2000

How to Use This Book

This book can be used in several ways.

1 Those of a methodical disposition may read it through from cover to cover.
2 Those who like a less 'linear' approach may follow the threads from author to author, tracing themes or styles of writing. I have indicated these by pointers at the bottom of the pages. So if you want to follow writers who have chosen strange subjects, it will be indicated thus:

☞ Unusual Subjects
Margaret Cavendish; Rev. Samuel Wesley; The Devout Salutationist; James Grainger; Rev. Cornelius Whur; James McIntyre; Solyman Brown; Francis Saltus Saltus

Finally, I have dared to give each writer a personal rating. This has been carefully worked out according to a complex rating system, with points awarded for improbable plotting, inadequate spelling, tortuous syntax, number of people dead or maimed, blatant self-promotion and general entertainment value. Points were, of course, added for terrible rhymes, but deducted for too much sentimentality. If the writer had an amusing name that helped a lot.

Here is a guide to the ratings:

* ☞ **Generally a dull writer**
  with a few inspired moments of true badness.

** ☞ **Interestingly bad,**
  or amusingly strange and bizarre.

*** ☞ **An expert practitioner,**
  genuinely bad, with moments of genius.

**** ☞ **These writers have achieved greatness.**
  They are the *grand cru* of awful writing.

***** ☞ **The peak of genius.**
  Suffice it to say that only one person has achieved
  a five star rating.

The Early Pioneers

*

George Wither (1588–1667)
'Wretched Wither'

The *Dictionary of National Biography* says of Wither that his work is 'mainly remarkable for its mass, fluidity and flatness. It usually lacks any genuine literary quality and often sinks into imbecilic doggerel.'

High praise indeed, but no more than he deserved.

Described by Jonathan Swift as a 'fanatical rhymer and intemperate puritan', Wither was the first truly bad poet of the modern era. Among his many fans were Alexander Pope, who once called him 'wretched Wither' and Dryden, who said that if his verses 'rhymed and rattled, all was well'. He was thrown into prison at least five times because of his writing – mainly for its libellous content rather than its terrible style, although it must have been a close run thing as to which of the two was more offensive.

Here, for example, is a typical verse from his metrical version of Song of Songs:

> Sister and espoused peer
> Those thy breasts, how fair they are
> Better be those dugs of thine [1]
> Than the most delicious wine.
> And thine ointments are
> Sweeter than all spices far.

It is not clear who he is addressing here. If, by 'peer', he means a member of the aristocracy then it appears a rather

[1] For some reason, breasts figure large in the mind of the truly bad poet. For that reason, I feel I should warn readers of a nervous and/or lascivious disposition that there is more of this sort of thing coming up. Much, much more…

forward manner of addressing a Duchess. If, on the other hand, by 'sister', he means his real sister, then I am glad I wasn't a member of his family.

Uniquely, Wither's badness saved his life. In 1643 he was captured by Royalists. Because of his puritanism (and perhaps because they were poetry-lovers) he was sentenced to death. However, Sir John Denham, the royalist poet, heard of his capture and petitioned the King for Wither's release. When the King asked him why, Sir John replied that 'so long as Wither lived, Denham would not be accounted the worst poet in England.' Wither was reprieved.

It was a wise decision. Sir John, for all his undoubted dullness[2] could never have come up with a verse like this:

> Her hair like gold did glister,
> Each eye was like a star;
> She did surpass her sister,
> Which passed all others far.
> She would me honey call,
> She'd – O she'd kiss me too.
> But now alas! she's left me
> Falero, lero loo.
>
> from 'I Loved a Lass'

A verse which illustrates one of the key principles of the bad rhymer – 'if in doubt make up some words to fit'. Or, to paraphrase Dryden, 'as long as it rhymes it stays in the poem'.

---

[2] Sir John may not have been a bad writer but he was certainly devious. When his father disinherited him because of his appalling gambling, Sir John immediately 'reformed', and to prove it, wrote a treatise against gambling. His father was so pleased he immediately reinstated the boy in his will. Naturally, immediately after his father's death, Sir John lost his entire inheritance at cards.

Bibliography

Works include:

Abuses Stript and Whipt, London, 1613
Wither's Motto, London, 1621
Hymns and Songs of the Church, London, 1623
The Scholar's Purgatory, London, 1625
Britain's Remembrancer, London, 1628

☞ Bosom Fanatics
J. Gordon Coogler; Francis Saltus Saltus; Théophile Marzials

☞ Falero-lero-loo, riddlety-diddlety poets
Rev. William Cook; James Whitcomb Riley;
Théophile Marzials

Sir Thomas Urquhart (c.1605–c.1660)
The Worst Mathematical Writer in the World

Sir Thomas Urquhart was a man driven by a profound sense of injustice. Nothing unusual in that, but combine it with eccentricity, lack of proportion, warped intellect and the utter inability to write, and you have a recipe for some marvellously bad writing.

Thomas was a bankrupt from the moment he came of age, inheriting from his father not only the ancient lands of Cromarty, but also massive debts and a set of rapacious creditors.

Fortunately for lovers of bad writing, Sir Thomas used this sense of injustice to spur him on and, over the course of about twenty years, he produced a wonderfully varied range of batty works, including a proposal for a new language, the most unintelligible mathematical treatise ever, and a genealogical tree showing all his descendants right back to Adam and Eve ... and beyond.

An ardent royalist, he was knighted by Charles I in 1641. In engravings he is depicted as a slight figure with flowing cavalier locks and moustache and goatee beard. His clothes are trimmed with lace and his shoes are dwarfed by enormous buckles apparently designed to resemble two large chrysanthemums.

Presumably he borrowed the clothes, for many of his possessions were seized by his grasping creditors, notably one named Leslie of Findrassie. In one tragic instance, Thomas had his entire library taken away. All his efforts to repurchase his books were unavailing; none were ever restored to him, except a few which he found in a neighbouring county.

In desperation he turned to writing. Indeed, 'desperate' is a good description of his first book, which was the rather dull and uninteresting *Epigrams*, published in 1641. They lack the essential weirdness and mystification that marks his best work, although I was struck by the line

The whitest lawne receives the deepest moale...

However, the publication of his next book, *The Trissotetras*, in 1645, marked a spectacular nadir in the history of maths. It purports to be 'a most exquisite table for resolving all manner of triangles', and at the bottom of the title page is the line:

Published for the benefit of those that are Mathematically affected.

This book is so bad that even the editors of Urquhart's complete works felt they had to apologize for including it:

Some apology may appear necessary, even to an Antiquarian club, for reprinting a work so apparently unintelligible and useless... There appears to have been a perverted ingenuity exercised in writing it, and I imagine that with some patience, the author's plan might be understood, but I doubt if any man would take the trouble...

The book begins with a baffling diagram showing lots of triangles. The text, however, goes beyond baffling, to break through into the realm of complete nonsense. The following is a typical extract:

In amblygonosphericalls, which admit both of an extrinsecall and intrinsecall demission of the perpendicular, nineteen severall parts are to be considered...

The axioms of plain triangles are four, viz. Rulerst, Eproso, Grediftal and Bagrediffiu.

The directory of this second axiome is Pubkegdaxesh, which declareth that there are seven enodandas grounded on it, to wit, four rectangular, Upalem, Ubeman, Ekarul, Egalem, and three obliquangular, Danarele, Xemenoro and Shenerolem.

With refreshing honesty, he admits that hardly anyone will understand him:

> The novelty of these words I know will seem strange to some, and to the eares of illiterate hearers sound like terms of conjuration...

So in order to help out he appends a handy 'Lexicidion' explaining these terms. Or it *would* be helpful if the definitions weren't more opaque than the terms themselves. 'Oppecathetall', for example, is explained thus:

> Said of those loxogonosphericals which have a datisterurgetick concordance in their datas of the same cathetopposites and verticall angles

While 'Equisolea' is defined as

> ...of the grand orthogonosphericall scheme

I hope that's all clear. Obscure, bizarre and written in a language entirely his own, the *Trissotetras* alone assures Urquhart's place in the pantheon of bad writers. But the valiant knight had more books up his sleeve. First, though, there was the little matter of the English Civil War. Disaster nearly struck when he was captured at Worcester in 1651, losing a large number of manuscripts. Thankfully, these were restored by a Captain Goodwin, who rescued his notes 'from the inexorable rage of Vulcan, to whom by a file of musquettiers it was consecrated, to afford smoak to their pipes of tobacco'.

Thus, in 1652 Urquhart, despite being imprisoned in the Tower of London, was able to publish *Pantochronochanon, or the Promptuary of Time*. In this he draws a family tree of the Urquharts, but whereas most family pedigrees go back, say, to the Norman Conquest, Urquhart's went further. Much, much further. Right back, to before Adam.

> God the father, son and Holy Ghost, who were from all eternity, did in time of nothing create red earth; of red earth framed Adam and of a rib out of the side of Adam fashioned Eve...

From there we move on up, via Enoch and Noah, to such completely fabricated characters as Phrenedon, who was lucky enough to be 'in the house of the Patriarch Abraham at the time of the destruction of Sodom and Gomorrah'. Remarkably, his grandson, Chronomos, married Carissa, who 'was sister-in-law to Istavon king of the Germans', thus proving that Germany goes back a lot longer than we think.

Meanwhile, further down the family line in 1503 BC, Urquhart solemnly informs us:

> Cainotomos took to wife Thymelica, the daughter of Bacchus, in recompence of his having accompanied him in the conquest of the Indies. Cainotomos in his return thence into Greece, passed through the territories of Israel, where being acquainted with Deborah the judge and Prophetess, he received from her a very rich jewell, which afterwards by one of his succession was presented to Pentasilea, that queen of the Amozons that assisted the Trojans against Agamemnon.

Greek gods, Hebrew prophetesses, Trojans, Amazons – this is a very cosmopolitan family. (They even had a son called Rodrigo, bringing in a nice Hispanic connection.) And so it goes on. Anybody who was anybody – and a great many people who were never anybody at all – was a part of the Urquhart dynasty. King Arthur, the founders of Ireland and Scotland, even Termuth, who in 1623 BC

> was that daughter of Pharaoh Amenophis which found Moses amongst the bulrushes, and brought him up as if he had been her own childe...

At the end a table points out he is the 143rd generation from Adam, the 134th from Noah. Not everyone's family tree stretches back to 5598 BC, nor can many of us number among their ancestors a small piece of red earth. At least, not with a straight face.

Given that most of the names in the family tree and most of the terms in *The Trissotetras* are invented, it is hardly surprising that Urquhart soon put his unique skills to work on inventing an entire language. He announced his intentions in his book called *The Jewel*, subtitled *The Discovery of a most exquisite JEWEL, more precious then Diamonds inchased in Gold, the like whereof was never seen in any age; found in the kennel of Worcester-streets, the day after the Fight, and six before the Autumnal Equinox, anno 1651:*

> *My Universal Language is a most exquisite jewel. It hath eleven genders, seven moods, four voices, ten cases, besides the nominative, and twelve parts of speech; every word signifieth as well backwards as forwards; and it is so compact of style that a single syllable will express the year, month, day, hour and partition of the hour.*

This new language promises many major upgrades on the old one, including:

> *Eighthly, Every word capable of number, is better provided therewith in this language then by any other for in stead of two or three numbers, which others have, this afordeth you four; to wit, the singular, duel, plural and redual.*

I don't know what he means by 'redual' and I'm by no means certain he knew either. However, he does promise a high degree of user-friendliness:

> *Each noun thereof, or verb, may begin or end with a vowel or consonant as to the peruser shall seem most expedient.*

And lovers of crossword puzzles will not be disappointed:

> *Every word in this language signifieth as well backward as forward, and however you invert the letter, still shall you fall upon significant words, whereby a wonderful facility is obtained in making of anagrams.*

Following the proposals there is a twenty-two-point argument claiming that 'a man hath a full right of propriety to the goods of his own mind', although who would want to steal the contents of Sir Thomas's mind is beyond me. He seems to be arguing that the idea of the Universal Language 'deserveth great sums of money'. Or to put it in Urquhart-speak:

if a malevolent time disobstetricate not their enixibility, it followeth
of necessity that he should reap the benefit that is due for the inven-
tion, with hopes of a higher remuneration for what of the like nature
remaineth unsatisfied.

The proposal for the Universal Language is combined with a
sort of biographical history of Scotland, showing how the

new Palestine as the kirkomanetick Philarchaists would have it called,
comes to be upbraided with the opproby of covetousness...

It is, apparently, a treatise defending the Scots against the
charge of avarice. Unfortunately, the impact of Urquhart's
defence is somewhat undermined by the obscurity of his
language and by the fact he spends the first and last pages of
the book appealing for money.

In 1653 Urquhart returned to the theme of the Universal
Language with *Logopandecteision or an Introduction to the
Universal Language*. It treads much the same ground as his
first work, although it is blessed with a lovely frontispiece
showing Sir Thomas sitting on a rock, while six maidens
offer him laurel crowns for 'judgment, learning, witt, invention, sweetness and stile'. Below the rock is a fountain, which
two more maidens appear to be cleaning with lavatory
brushes. Meanwhile, above Sir Thomas a winged horse flies
by, lying, for some strange reason, on its side. Perhaps one of
its wings wasn't working.

The book is split into six chapters called 'Neaudethaumata',
'Chrestasebeia', 'Cleronomaporia', 'Chyseomystes', 'Neleo-
dicastes' and 'Philoponauxesis'. Only the first chapter,
'Neaudethaumata', is about the 'wonders of the new speech'.
The rest of the chapters are about, respectively, 'the impious
dealing of creditors', 'the intricacy of a distressed successor or
apparent heir', 'the Covetous Preacher', 'the Pitiless Judge' and
'the furtherance of industry' – which is basically a demand for
money in order to bring the universal language into existence.

However, the main body of the book ends with a charming little verse, which shows that, had he really turned his
mind to it, he could have been a superbly bad poet as well:

> *Of Postulatas a sursolid, whose*
> *Content doth twice that square of squares inclose,*
> *Which is the double of the cube of two,*
> *Is here display'd for the' Author's sake, to shew*
> *How that square dealing will him best become,*
> *Whereby he gets his own in solidum.*

Before we quite reach the end of the book, he slips in another thirty-two-point argument for money and the restitution of his lands.

Unfortunately, all his appeals were in vain. When he got back to Scotland he found that his creditors had seized all his property, under the belief that he had perished at Worcester. He fled to London and thence to the Continent.

It is Sir Thomas's unique writing style that secures his place amongst the greats. No one before, or after him, has used words with more eloquence, grandeur and complete obscurity. Not that he saw it this way. As far as he was concerned he was writing for the layman:

> *Why, I could truly have enlarged my discourse with a choicer variety of phrase, and made it overflow the field of the readers understanding, with an inundation of greater eloquence ... schematologetically adorning the proposed theme with the most especial and chief flowers of the garden of rhetoric... I could have introduced, in case of obscurity, synonymal, exargastic and palilogetic elucidations; for sweetness of phrase, antimetathetic commutations of epithets; for the vehement excitation of a matter, exclamation in the front, and epiphonemas in the rear. I could have used, for the promptlier stirring up of passion, apostrophal and prosopopoeial diversions; and, for the appeasing and settling of them, some epanorthotic revocations and aposiopetic restraints... But I hold it now expedient, without further ado, to stop the current of my pen... and write with simplicity.*

Urquhart died in 1660. According to legend, he expired suddenly in 'a fit of excessive laughter, on being informed by his servant that Charles the Second had been restored to the throne'. He may have been poor, exiled and dispossessed. But at least he died happy.

Bibliography

*The Works of Sir Thomas Urquhart of Cromarty, Knight,
Edinburgh 1834* Presented to the Maitland Club by Sylvester
Douglas Stirling of Glenbervie

☞ Made-Up Words and Strange Syntax
'Lord' Timothy Dexter; Leopold John Manners De Michele;
Théophile Marzials; Pedro Carolino; Nancy Luce; Amanda
McKittrick Ros

☞ Philosophy and Theology
Margaret Cavendish; The Devout Salutationist; 'Lord'
Timothy Dexter; Eliza Cook; William Nathan Stedman;
Keith Odo Newman

****

Margaret Cavendish, Duchess of Newcastle (1624–74)

Poet, Novelist, Philosopher, Food-obsessive

A strange thing has happened to the reputation of Margaret Cavendish, Duchess of Newcastle. She has become an icon. She is now praised in some academic circles as an early feminist author, whose work demonstrates 'the empowering possibilities of disguise or masking for women'.

What her work actually demonstrates is the empowering possibilities of bad writing, especially when allied to an eccentric personality and an imagination that makes Salvador Dali seem like an accountant.

Born in Essex in 1623, she became a maid of honour to Queen Henrietta Maria, marrying William Cavendish, Duke of Newcastle in 1644. An ardent royalist, the Duke was forced into exile after the unfortunate shortening of King Charles I. On the restoration of the monarchy, Margaret returned to England and it was there that she began to publish for the first time.

Of course, praise must be given to her for even trying. In the seventeenth century it was rare for a woman to publish anything at all, let alone put her name to it. And given the quality of what she wrote, putting her name to it appears an even braver move.

She is also to be praised for the range of her writing. She did not just restrict herself to bad verse; no, she wrote bad plays, bad prose and even bad philosophy. Although unhampered by the trappings of an education, she was much given to scientific speculation and concocted several intriguing theories, including one which claimed that some people lived longer because their atoms were packed closer together.

She was a true eccentric, given to acts of personal excess and sporting a dress sense that caused crowds to gather wherever she appeared. After reading her first book, *Poems and Fancies*, Dorothy Osborne remarked that 'there are many soberer people in bedlam'. In later years, Virginia Woolf called her 'a vision of loneliness and riot... As if some giant cucumber had spread itself all over the roses and carnations in the garden and choked them to death.'[1]

Her poetry was often dictated to servants in the middle of the night – which might explain why so much of it was about food. She was obviously peckish and it is a sobering thought that if she'd had a fridge in her room we might have been spared such gems as 'Posset for Nature's Breakfast', which begins with possibly the worst opening line in all poetry:

> *Life scums the cream of Beauty with Time's spoon.*

It is not easy to write a poem which compares nature to a full English breakfast, but Margaret succeeds triumphantly, especially in the line which compares 'fair and bashful eyes' to a pair of eggs – presumably fried.

In 'Death, The Cook Of Nature' we find her considering the more sombre aspects of gastronomy:

> *Death is the cook of Nature; and we find*
> *Meat dressèd several ways to please her mind.*
> *Some meats she roasts with fevers, burning hot,*
> *And some she boils with dropsies in a pot.*
> *Some for jelly consuming by degrees,*
> *And some with ulcers, gravy out to squeeze.*
> *Some flesh as sage she stuffs with gouts, and pains,*
> *Others for tender meat hangs up in chains.*
> *Some in the sea she pickles up to keep,*
> *Others, as brawn is soused, those in wine steep.*

Once she has hit upon the idea of Death as a mad chef, the metaphors get more and more repulsive:

[1] An unusual metaphor and one that almost elevates Virginia herself to the ranks of the truly bad writers. It is not easy to shake off the image of Margaret Cavendish as a giant cucumber, writhing through the vegetable patch and causing havoc in the petunias.

In sweat sometimes she stews with savoury smell,
A hodge-podge of diseases tasteth well.

And it is not long before Death is more *charcutier* than cook:

Then Death cuts throats, for blood-puddings to make,
And puts them in the guts, which colics rack.

'Nature's Dessert' is similarly food-oriented, being an ambitious attempt to liken the whole of life to a meal, in which the 'Biscuits of Love' crumble away in the face of the 'jelly of fear' and a cheese of 'fresh green-sickness'.

However, she was more than merely a poet, even a poet obsessed with a fry-up. She was also a natural philosopher. Consider her poetical meditation 'What is Liquid?'[2]

All that doth flow we cannot liquid name,
Or else would fire and water be the same;
But that is liquid which is moist and wet;
Fire that propriety can never get…

Say what you like about the limitations of Margaret's science, but she's hit the nail on the head here; no one has ever discovered wet fire.

Turning to her prose, we find her inability has flowered into some of the most obscure plots ever imagined. In *Assaulted and Pursued Chastity*, for example, we follow the adventures of a shipwrecked young woman who falls into the clutches of a prince – 'a grand monopolizer of young virgins'. Just as he is preparing to dishonour her, she persuades his accomplice that a wizard once advised her to shoot a gun on her birthday for good luck. Accordingly she is lent a pistol, which she uses to shoot the prince.

To you or I, being shot by somebody might be a bit of a turn-off; but the prince is made of sterner stuff. He views this assassination attempt as merely playing hard to get, and once

[2] Who of us can claim we have not spent many a sleepless night pondering the question 'What is Liquid?' (Or at least, the related question 'What was that liquid and how much of it did I drink?')

his wounds have healed he redoubles his efforts. She craftily takes poison to avoid his advances, but is revived by his aunt and escapes disguised as a boy.

At this point the story leaves gritty realism behind and enters the world of fantasy. In her new guise as a lad called Travellia, she is shipwrecked again and encounters a race of purple-skinned humans with white hair and black teeth. (However, just to make sure that the social niceties are preserved, all the nobility are coloured orange. This, it strikes me, is an easier way of recognizing the upper classes than asking them what school they went to.) Although they are about to sacrifice her, she manages once again to cadge a gun off someone and shoots the high priest. She then becomes their leader and returns home.

It never rains but it pours, however, and on the way home she is once again captured by the randy prince, who has become a pirate. After yet more shipwrecked adventures, they end up as generals of opposing armies and have to fight a duel.[3] This time she is wounded – perhaps because she couldn't find anyone to lend her a gun – although she soon recovers her spirits and sings:

> Then Life is Pain and Pain is only Life
> Which is a Motion, Motion all is strife;
> As forward, backward, up or down, or so
> Sideways, or in a circle round doth go.

This poem – which also sums up Margaret's plots – seems to be arguing that if you want to remain happy you should just stop moving about. However, this option is not available to poor Travellia, who after numerous other flights, battles and philosophical musings eventually reveals that she is in fact a woman. In response to this revelation, the army rather chivalrously cries 'Heaven bless you, of what sex soever you be'. After that, everybody marries and virtue is rewarded.

[3] I have to admit that, although I have read this passage several times, I have no idea how this happens.

It ought to be pointed out that Margaret had a serious purpose in mind when she wrote this story. 'My endeavour,' she revealed, 'was to show young women the danger of travelling without their parents, husbands, or particular friends to guard them.'

In this I think she is particularly successful. I am sure that if more young women knew that they might be abducted by princes, caught up in shipwrecks and almost sacrificed by purple-skinned savages, they would take more care with their travel arrangements. Or at the very least invest in a gun of their own so they don't have to keep borrowing one.

For those to whom the plot of *Assaulted and Pursued Chastity* is too dull, Margaret's other famous work, *The Description of a New World, Called the Blazing World* offers more satisfying fare.

On page one a young lady sails to the North Pole, where all her crew-mates die but she is kept alive by 'the light of her beauty, the heat of youth and the protection of the gods'. And, presumably, a good sleeping bag. By page three the pace has hotted up and she has encountered talking bears, half-human foxes and men shaped like geese. Eventually she arrives at court.

> *No sooner was the lady brought before the Emperor, but he conceived her to be some goddess, and offered to worship her; which she refused, telling him (for by that time she had pretty well learned their language) that although she came out of another world, yet was she but a mortal; at which the Emperor, rejoicing, made her his wife, and gave her an absolute power to rule and govern all that world as she pleased.*

Now that's what you call a whirlwind romance. Suffice it to say that the book is a milestone in the history of truly bad prose. As one critic has written:

> *Few works of Science-fiction can equal the confused, ridiculous fantasy of the Blazing World. As either narrative or speculation it is quite hopeless; the absurd action, the ludicrous situations and the tedious quasi-philosophical speculations make it unbearably dull...*

And those are its good points. The whole thing reads as if Margaret has been overdosing on the Biscuits of Love, the Cheese of Green-Sickness and the After-Dinner Mints Of Severely Delusional Behaviour.

Her plays, on the other hand, go to the opposite extreme, eschewing entertainment for supreme dullness. Ignoring the narrow, petty conventions that insist on a play having a beginning, a middle and an end, she constructed her dramas to a plan entirely her own:

> Some of my scenes have no acquaintance or relation to the rest of the scenes, although in one and the same play; which is the reason many of my plays will not end as other plays do.

Her plays are as random, chaotic and, it must be said, undramatic as real life. Sadly, none were ever performed, mainly due to their extreme length. Act V, Scene 15 of 'Death's Banquet', for example, consists of one character delivering a speech of nearly 6,000 words. Small wonder that she thought her plays 'might tire the spectators, who are forced or bound by the rules of civility to sit out a play; if they be not sick.' Frankly, civility doesn't come into it. There would be few spectators who, when faced with the prospect of one of Margaret's plays wouldn't immediately fake scarlet fever, or get a note from their mum.

Take 'The Sociable Companions or the Female Wits', which was published in her *Plays, Never Before Printed* (1668). The prologue warns of the delights in store:

> Noble spectators our Authoress doth say
> She doth believe you will condemn her play.
> Here's no design, no plot, nor any ground,
> Foundation none, nor any to be found...

This is not exactly a 'hard sell',[4] but at least she's honest. The play begins with two soldiers discussing how they are to live,

---

[4] Her first collection, *Plays* (1662), has eleven pages of 'Letters to the Readers' at the beginning, which repeatedly warn readers that 'most of my plays would seem tedious upon the stage'. Never mind the stage, they are hardly a barrel of laughs in a book.

now that they have left the army and more, particularly, how they are to be cured of the pox. As the Captain so poetically puts it:

CAPT: *How shall our Pocky bodies live if we be Cashier'd?*

However, the Pocky Captain is not left worrying for long. Within minutes a student called Will Fullwit[5] has feigned death, and then attacked him with a sword, although it is never made clear exactly why. Will says it is the result of 'seeing a new play'. Probably it was one of Margaret's which is enough to induce anyone to attack people. After that, the unfortunately named Dick Traveller enters, who has been to the 'Pole in Greenland' and whose hair has, as a consequence, turned white.

The plot, as far as I can make out, tells of their hunt for riches and wives. Along the way they visit several taverns, have a number of completely baffling conversations and attend a 'spiritual court' where a moneylender called 'Get-All' is accused of impregnating a woman by 'having an idea'.

WILL: *I am absolutely of the opinion that the Idea of Man, by the help of a strong imagination, may beget a Child; which is sufficiently proved; for she, seeing Mr. Get-all enter into the house of Mr. Inkhorn the Scrivener, viewed his person so exactly that when she was in bed, a strong imagination seized on her, by which she conceived a Child.*

This is a worrying theory. If imagination can get you pregnant, then we are all at risk,[6] and the mind is filled with visions of people having to wear condoms on their heads like balaclavas. However, it all turns out to be a trick and everything ends happily although I couldn't tell you eactly how.

Plays, Never Before Printed also contains a fragment called *A Piece of a Play*, which Margaret originally intended to accompany *The Blazing World*. It features Sir Puppy Dogman,

---

[5] 'Will Halfwit' might be a better name.
[6] Apart, of course, from accountants.

Monsieur Ass, Ladies Eagle, Sparrow, Titmouse and Woodcock, Lord Monkey and my own favourite, Mr Worm-Man. She must have had some seriously bad cheese that evening.

To be fair, Margaret is not always bad. There are times when her work hits the heights of mediocrity (at which point we lose interest). And in an age where women were expected to 'know their place', she is to be commended for breaking the boundaries, for pushing herself forward and thrusting her tremendous lack of ability into the limelight for future generations to appreciate.

The academics are right, albeit for the wrong reasons. Margaret Cavendish was a pioneer. She paved the way for the great female inept authors that were to follow. She showed just what a powerful imagination can do when harnessed to a complete lack of self-discipline and an empty stomach. It is noticeable that much of her work shows women battling against the odds to gain status, recognition and power – even if it is only from purple people with black teeth and men shaped like geese.

Finally, she always had the assurance that only the truly great bad writers have, that there is a huge audience somewhere for their work.

> I wish I had a thousand, or rather ten thousand millions [of readers] … nay, that their number were infinite, that the issue of my brain, fame, and name might live to eternity if it were possible.

Whatever others might say, she was convinced of her own genius:

> I am not covetous, but as ambitious as ever any of my sex was, is, or can be; which makes that though I cannot be Henry the Fifth, or Charles the Second, yet I endeavour to be Margaret the First…

Bibliography

Poems and Fancies, London, 1653; 2nd ed., London, 1654; 3rd. ed., London, 1668
Philosophical Fancies, London, 1653
Nature's Pictures, London, 1656
Plays, London, 1662
Plays, Never Before Printed, London, 1668
Observations Upon Experimental Philosophy, to which is added, The Description of a New World Called the Blazing World, London, 1668

☞ Novels and Fiction
Nikolai Chernyshevsky; Shepherd M. Dugger; Amanda McKittrick Ros

☞ Philosophy and Theology
The Devout Salutationist; 'Lord' Timothy Dexter; Eliza Cook; Thomas Wirgman; William Nathan Stedman; Keith Odo Newman

☞ Unusual Subjects
Rev. Samuel Wesley; The Devout Salutationist; James Grainger; Rev. Cornelius Whur; James McIntyre; Solyman Brown; Francis Saltus Saltus; Nancy Luce

☞ Four Stars and Over
Pedro Carolino; Shepherd M. Dugger; Joseph Gwyer; William MacGonagall; James McIntyre; Théophile Marzials; Julia Moore; Walter Reynolds; Francis Saltus Saltus

***

'The Devout Salutationist' (fl. 1668)

A Devout Salutation of the Holy Members of the Body of the Glorious Mother of God, was published in Paris in 1668 and consists of meditations on all the parts of the body of the Virgin Mary. Nothing is known of the anonymous monk who was the author of this work, although judging by the evidence he was probably spending far too much time on his own in his cell.

'Religion, decency and good sense are equally struck at by such an extravagance,' wrote one critic, and it is not hard to see why. The author takes each bodily part of the Virgin Mary in turn and draws a meaningful moral from them.

The Salutation to the Hair runs:

> I salute you, charming hair of Maria! Rays of the mystical sun! Lines of the centre and circumference of all created perfection! Veins of gold of the mine of love![1] Chains of the prison of God! Roots of the tree of life! Rivulets of the fountain of Paradise! Strings to the bow of Charity! Nets that caught Jesus and shall be used in the hunting-day of souls.

Whilst he salutes the ears in a novel fashion:

> I salute ye, intelligent ears of Maria! ye presidents of the princes of the poor! Tribunal for their petitions; salvation at the audience of the miserable! University of all Divine Wisdom!... Ye are pierced with the ring of our chains; ye are impearled with our necessities.

Mary was certainly unique in many ways, but no one has ever commented on her intelligent ears before. Indeed, as the

---

[1] The author seems to be implying that Mary has blonde hair, which is unusual for a Jewish girl.

author says later in the paragraph, they are so intelligent, they have formed their own university.

Isaac D'Israeli, who translated these passages, called them 'two of the most decent of these salutations'. I hate to think what the others are like.

Bibliography

Dévotes Salutations des Membres sacres du Corps de la Glorieuse Vièrge, Mère de Dieu, Paris, 1668

☞ Unusual Subjects
Margaret Cavendish; Rev. Samuel Wesley; James Grainger; Rev. Cornelius Whur; James McIntyre; Solyman Brown; Francis Saltus Saltus; Nancy Luce

Curious Book Titles

The seventeenth century brought us many innovations, including newspapers, coffee and beheading your monarch. It was a time when writers really began to let themselves go, sometimes with impressively bad results.

In the field of book titles especially, they began to develop a taste for the ornate, the complicated, the downright weird. The Puritan authors in particular took a wonderfully imaginative approach to their book titles. Food features heavily:

> *Eggs of Charity, layed by the Chickens of Covenant, and boiled with the Water of Divine Love. Take Ye and eat.*

> *The Spiritual Mustard pot, to make the Soul Sneeze with Devotion.*

And, rather tastefully,

> *Spiritual Milk for Babes, drawn out of the Breasts of Both Testaments for their Soul's Nourishment*

Some are more what you might call 'argumentative':

> *A Shot aimed at the Devil's Hind-Quarters through the Tube of the Cannon of Covenant*

> *Tobacco battered, and the Pipes shattered about their Ears that idly idolize so loathsome a Vanity, by a Volley of holy shot thundered from Mount Helicon: a poem against the use of tobacco by Joshua Sylvester.*

Whilst several appeal to our sense of smell:

> *A most Delectable Sweet Perfumed Nosegay for God's Saints to Smell at.*

> *Seven Sobs of a Sorrowful Soul for Sin, or the Seven Penitential Psalms of the Princely Prophet David; whereunto are also added,*

William Humius's Handful of Honeysuckles, and Divers Godly and Pithy Ditties, now newly augmented.

My favourite, however, brings together a number of unusual elements:

A Reaping-Hook, well tempered, for the Stubborn Ears of the coming Crop; or, Biscuit baked in the Oven of Charity, carefully conserved for the Chickens of the Church, the Sparrows of the Spirit, and the sweet Swallows of Salvation.

Of course, I don't know if this is the work of a genuinely bad writer, but anyone who can bring together farming implements, biscuit production and a range of common birds has obviously got potential.

Reverend Samuel Wesley (1660–1735)

Father of John and Charles and Atrocious Poet

One of the things that marks out the truly bad poet, as opposed to the merely 'quite bad', is the ambition of their subject matter. Not for them the normal subjects such as love, death, friendship, royalty or cats.

No, the truly bad poet is a pioneer. He or she writes on manure, dairy products or dead puppies.[1] And no one has more consciously tried to break new ground than Samuel Wesley, father of the more famous John and Charles.

In his youth he was a schoolmate of Daniel Defoe, who was later to write the novels *Robinson Crusoe* and *Moll Flanders*. Happily, no trace of Daniel's talent rubbed off on his school chum.

Samuel's major work – and the book on which his reputation as a bad writer rests – is charmingly entitled *Maggots: Or, Poems On Several Subjects, Never Before Handled*. Published in 1685, and engagingly illustrated with a picture of the author with a large maggot sitting on his forehead, *Maggots* takes verse into a brave new world of obscure and ludicrous themes.

His opening 'Epistle to the Reader' begins with a somewhat ungenerous warning:

Gentle Reader,

In the first place, pray notice this is addressed only to those that buy the Book, for such as only borrow't, my good Friend the Bookseller and I will ha' nothing to do with 'em.

---

[1] Not literally, obviously. Most publishers would turn their noses up at anything submitted on a dead puppy. Even a poodle.

Having made his stand against piracy, he goes on to assure the reader that 'all here are my own pure Maggots, the natural issue of my brain-pan'. He is stating the obvious. Not only would no one else have thought of these poems, only Samuel would actually want to.

Poems such as 'On a Cow's Tail', 'Three Skips of a Louse', 'On The Bear-Fac'd Lady' and 'An Anacreontique on a Pair of Breeches' demonstrate not only a challenging idea of what a poem should be about, but verse styles which fully live down to their subject matter. 'On two Souldiers killing one another for a Groat' demonstrates his complete lack of mastery of basic rhymes:

> Full doleful Tales have oft been told,
> By Chimney warm in Winter cold,
> About the Sacred Thirst of Gold;
> To hear 'em half 'twould mad ye.
> To Jayl how many headlong run,
> How many a hopeful Youth's undone,
> How many a vile, ungracious Son,
> For this has murder'd Daddy?

Whilst the wonderfully titled 'A Tame Snake left in a Box of Bran, was devoured by Mice after a great Battle' shows how 'different' his subject matter could be.

> A little Box which his kind Master gave,
> His Pallace was, and would have been his Grave;
> But sacriligious Mouths him thence did tear,
> And made their Guts his loathed Sepulcher.

He is very fond of narrative poems, particularly those describing unusual events. The title of one poem more or less sums up the entire plot:

> A covetous old Fellow having taken occasion to hang himself a little; another comes in, in the nick, and cuts him down; but instead of Thanking him for his Life, he accuses him for spoyling the Rope.

A particular favourite of mine is the charming verse entitled, with a glorious lack of both taste and grammar, 'On a Supper of Stinking Ducks'. He supplies the story behind this poem as follows:

> *The Story thus – At a club of Younkers, after a Frost a couple of Wild Ducks were brought. A thaw coming the day after, these having before been frozen hard, fell in, appear'd all black, and stunk most harmoniously – yet, that nothing good might be wasted, the Purchasers dress't 'em, and eat the first pretty nimbly, not staying to tast it; but by that time, Colon being a little pacifi'd, advancing to the second, it drove 'em all off, and was given a decent burial at last in the Boghouse.*

If that isn't a proper subject for poetry, then I don't know what is. Having given this heart-warming precis, the poem graphically illustrates its subject matter.

> *O Spirits of Arm-pits, and Essence of Toes!*
> *O Hogo of Ulcers, and Hospital Nose!*
> *…*
> *With fat blubby Pease that are grimy all o're,*
> *Thick butter'd with delicate matter and Gore!*

Given the nature of the subject matter, it is sometimes hard for the reader to believe that this man was a clergyman and father of two of the most influential religious leaders of the modern age. One cannot imagine either John or Charles using the kind of language that their father uses in the poem 'On a Discourteous Damsel that call'd the right Worshipful Author – (an't please ye!) Saucy Puppy'.

> *Ugly! Ill-natur'd! impudent and proud!*
> *Sluttish! nonsensical! and idly loud!*
> *Thy name's a ranker Scandal to my Pen,*
> *Than al thy words could be spew'd up agen.*
> *…*
> *E'ne get a Mask, or with thy Visage daunted,*
> *The Londoners will swear their streets are haunted:*

Below the Plague, below the Pox and Itch,
Take your own farewell, you're a Sawcy Bitch.

His finest poem, with a title which should thrill all lovers of bad verse, is called 'A Pindaricque on the Grunting of a Hog'.

The 'pindaric' – a verse form characterized by irregular line length and arbitrary rhymes[2] – is first pictured soaring through the air looking for a subject to settle on:

Now out of sight she flys,
Roving with gaudy wings,
A-cross the stormy skys,
Then down again,
Her self she Flings,
Without uneasiness or Pain
To Lice, and Dogs,
To Cows, and Hogs
And follows their melodious grunting
o'er the Plain.

Having decided to celebrate the noisy pig, the poet has to reassure the animal with promises of vegetarianism:

Harmonious Hog draw near!
No bloody butchers here
Thou needst not fear.

Like all great artists, Samuel is not afraid to tackle the taboo subjects. Hence the hint of cannibalism in verse three:

Dear Hog! Thou king of meat!
So near thy Lord Mankind,
The nicest taste can scarce a difference find!

'Nicest' in this sense meant 'delicate' or 'sophisticated', although it is hard to see what is particularly delicate about someone failing to tell the difference between the taste of pig flesh and human beings.

[2] Thus making it an ideal verse form for bad poets, who are naturally inclined to ignore such trivialities as rhyme schemes and regular rhythm.

The poem is not over until the fat pig sings, however, and in a stirring climax the poet waits agog for the finale:

> Harmonious Hog draw near, and from thy beauteous
>   Snowt
>   Whilst we attend with Ear
>   Like thine prik't up devout,
> To taste thy sugary Voice, which here, and there,
> With wanton Curls, Vibrates around the Circling Air,
> Harmonous Hog! Warble some Anthem out!

Few people would find pig warbling so attractive or uplifting. But that, surely, is what makes Samuel a genius.

Samuel never again reached the peak of *Maggots*. He served as a vicar for almost forty years, spent some time in jail for non-payment of debts and wrote a commentary on the Book of Job which has the rare gift of making the reader suffer almost as much as Job himself.

In 1713 he published a long poem, *An Hymn on Peace, to the Prince of Peace*. Although this is a pedestrian piece of work in comparison with *Maggots*, it does contain a nice opening which seems to plead for a more tolerant audience:

> Once more, O Saviour Prince, thy Bard inspire,
> Instruct his Hands to touch the Sacred Lyre,
> With notes like those which calm'd the Hebrew King,
> And let none throw the Javelin while I sing.

Quite what effect his writing had on his sons it is hard to say. There are those who think that John Wesley only founded Methodism as a way of saying 'sorry' for his father's poetry. And when the great preacher was banned from preaching within Anglican churches, he dramatically preached upon his father's grave.[3]

Charles, meanwhile, became one of the greatest hymn writers.[4] Perhaps he took after his mother.

---

[3] As opposed to lovers of poetry, who merely dance on it.
[4] Although even he had his moments. See 'Hymns Ancient and Appalling'. pp. 56–9.

Bibliography

Maggots – or Poems on several Subjects Never before Handled,
   London, 1685
An Hymn on Peace, to the Prince of Peace, London, 1713

☞ Unusual Subjects

Margaret Cavendish; The Devout Salutationist; James
Grainger; Rev. Cornelius Whur; James McIntyre; Solyman
Brown; Francis Saltus Saltus; Nancy Luce

***

James Grainger (1721–67)
Poet of Manure

There can have been few ordeals more terrifying in the world of eighteenth-century literature than having to read out one of your poems to Dr Johnson. And it must have been even worse if, like James Grainger, you wrote largely about manure.

James Grainger MD is primarily known for his poem *The Sugar Cane*, an epic work in four books which covers the cultivation, harvest and refining of sugar, as practised in the West Indies in the eighteenth century. In 1758, after a career as a physician in the army and in fashionable London, Dr Grainger went to the West Indies and settled at Basseterre on the island of St Christopher. Here he realized, with the vision of a true pioneer, that no one had ever written a poem about sugar cane. Of course, some would argue that there was a good reason for this omission i.e. it's a terrible subject for poetry. But Grainger was not to be put off. He set to work and, as an early editor wrote, 'Sometime before the publication of his poem he revisited England, and submitted the manuscript to the correction of his literary friends...'

The 'friends' in this case were Dr Johnson and his circle. The reading went swimmingly until Grainger came to the start of a new stanza and, before the greatest critics of the eighteenth century, read out the immortal line:

Now Muse, let's sing of rats.

Naturally, the assembled company behaved with gentility and decorum. Apart, that is, from the hysterical laughter.[1]

[1] What made it worse was that someone looked over his shoulder and saw that the verse originally ran 'Now muse, let's sing of mice', but he'd changed it to rats as he thought that they were more poetic.

Our more refined eyes can appreciate the poem for its true badness. Particularly for its continued celebration of manure. Grainger is keen on all aspects of sugar-cane production, but reserves some of his most moving verse for all aspects of soil fertilization. He is the Wordsworth of waste products, the Shelley of soil-improvement.

> *Of composts shall the Muse disdain to sing?*
> *Nor soil her heavenly plumes?*

he cries, before advising the planter

> *Then planter, wouldst thou double thine estate,*
> *Never, ah! never, be asham'd to tread*
> *Thy dung-heaps.*

Timely advice to us all, although I would recommend you also wipe your feet. If I have a criticism, it is that he remains frustratingly imprecise on the finer detail of compost application:

> *Whether the fattening compost in each hole*
> *'Tis best to throw, or on the surface spread,*
> *Is undetermin'd: trials must decide.*

Meanwhile, he debates the thorny issue of yams:

> *Some of the skillful teach, and some deny*
> *That yams improve the soil. In meagre lands*
> *'Tis known the yam will ne'er to bigness swell;*
> *And from each mould the vegetable tribes,*
> *However frugal, nutriment derive...*

Who, or what, the 'vegetable tribes' are, I can't imagine. Possibly eighteenth-century environmentalists.

Book II begins promisingly,

> *Enough of culture.[2] – A less pleasing theme,*
> *What ills await the ripening cane, demands*
> *My serious numbers.*

---

[2] A motto many of our worst writers would subscribe to.

And he goes on to expatiate at length on the diseases that attack sugar cane, even though it is, as he once again reminds us, 'well-manur'd'.

Book III is largely about sugar production and tells how 'the cane,/ Whose juice now longs to murmur down the spout' eagerly awaits the winter. In Book IV he spends a considerable amount of time on the care and maintenance of slaves:

> One precept more, it imports to know.
> The Blacks, who drink the Quanza's lucid stream,
> Fed by ten thousand streams, are prone to bloat…

As if the prospect of bloated Blacks isn't bad enough, here is his advice on how to manage your 'Ethiops':

> Wouldst thou secure thine Ethiop from those ails,
> Which change of climate, change of waters breed,
> And food unusual? let Machaon draw
> From each some blood, as age and sex require;
> And well with vervain, well with sempre-vive,
> Unload their bowels.

'Unloading your slaves' bowels' strikes me as verging on the inhumane, and is probably an infringement of basic human rights, but at least he is a strong advocate of warm clothing:

> To every negro, as the candle-weed
> Expands his blossoms to the cloudy sky,
> And moist Aquarius melts in daily showers;
> A woolly vestment give…

Grainger, it is obvious, is a poet of *real* life in the Caribbean. Not for him the clichéd sandy beaches, blue seas and coconut palms. No, his Caribbean is a world of rats and compost and, above all, intestinal disease:

> Yet of the ills which torture Libya's sons,
> Worms tyrannize the worst.

Even his other famous work, the 'beautiful ballad of *Bryan and Pereene*',' was founded on a real incident. A tender, moving love story, it tells of a lover so keen to see his beloved again that he leaps from the boat and swims to the shore.

> *The north-west wind did briskly blow,*
> *The ship was safely moor'd,*
> *Young Bryan thought the boat's crew slow,*
> *And so leap'd over board.*

Alas, never was the phrase 'look before you leap' more true. Bryan, unwittingly, has entered a Steven Spielberg film. He has almost reached his sweetheart when disaster strikes:

> *Then through the white surf did she haste*
> *To clasp her lovely swain;*
> *When ah! a shark bit through his waist;*
> *His heart's blood dy'd the main!*
>
> *He shriek'd! his half sprung from the wave,*
> *Streaming with purple gore,*
> *And soon it found a living grave,*
> *And, ah! was seen no more.*

Let's face it, in Grainger's world, if the worms don't get you, the sharks will.

Grainger was no stranger to disparagement and ridicule. His response to Tobias Smollett's criticism sounds a warning note to any writer who has the temerity to mock his work:

> *Thus the reader may discern how easy it is to turn into ridicule the most glowing descriptions, when one is in the humour of it, til he wheezes again at his own dull jest. But beautiful imagery strongly painted, will be poetry still and outlive any petulant attempt to make it ridiculous.*

I take the point. On the other hand, anyone who can write 'Now Muse, let's sing of rats' deserves all he gets.

Bibliography

Letter to Tobias Smollett MD occasioned by his criticism upon a late translation of Tibulus by Dr. Grainger, London, 1759

The Sugar-Cane: A Poem in Four Books With Notes, Dublin, 1766

The Poetical Works of James Grainger, 2 vols, Edinburgh, 1836

☞ Unusual Subjects

Margaret Cavendish; Rev. Samuel Wesley; The Devout Salutationist; Rev. Cornelius Whur; James McIntyre; Solyman Brown; Francis Saltus Saltus; Nancy Luce

The Five Golden Rules of Bad Writing
1. 'Heart' Is More Important Than 'Art'

Bad writers are often characterized by their good intentions. Never mind that they can't spell, can't rhyme, cannot, in fact, master any of the basic techniques of creative writing, they meant well. And as everybody knows, it's the thought that counts.

For example...
Ella Wheeler Wilcox, a supremely bad writer who didn't quite make it into this book, wrote:

> And it is not the poet's song, though sweeter than sweet bell's
>   chiming,
> Which thrills us through and through, but the heart which
>   beats under the rhyming.
> And therefore I say again, though I am art's one true lover,
> That it is not art, but heart, which wins the wide world over.

Ella used to go and recite her poems to the soldiers in the trenches during World War I – perhaps the only experience that would make the Battle of the Somme a preferable alternative.

The Spreading Flame

'Lord' Timothy Dexter (1747–1806) and Jonathan Plummer

The Greatest Philosopher of All the Known World (and his Poet Laureate)

'Lord' Timothy Dexter was a true original. He was a businessman, philosopher and philanthropist, as well as being the worst speller ever.

As a writer, his fame rests mainly on one deeply eccentric work – *A Pickle to the Knowing Ones*, which he published in 1802 and in which, with due modesty and humility, he described himself as 'First in the East, First in the West, and the greatest Philosopher of all the Known World'.[1]

The book is both Dexter's philosophy and his autobiography, all told in a style quite his own. Here is how he relates his momentous birth:

> *I was born when grat powers Rouled I was borne in 1747 Janeuarey 22 on this day in the morning A grat snow storme – the sines in the seventh house wives; mars Came fored – Joupeter stud by holding the Candel – I was to be one grat man.*[2]

Dexter lived for most of his life in Newburyport, New England. Starting as a leather dresser, making gloves and breeches, he became rich through a currency speculation during the depression of the late 1780s. He invested the wealth in a splendid house and in a number of increasingly strange trading adventures which all seemed to come off. He sent warming pans to the West Indies, where the natives used them as long-handled frying pans; and mittens to Jamaica, where Baltic traders bought them in delight and

---

[1] In a fit of humility, he may later have modified the second part to the phrase 'In the Western World'.
[2] Try reading it aloud. It doesn't help much but it's great fun.

sent them on to Europe. He even sent coal to Newcastle, where his consignment was in high demand as it arrived in the middle of a strike.

At the height of his fame and his riches he employed his own poet, one Jonathan Plummer, whose verse is clumsy enough to admit him to the minor leagues of bad poetry. It is a unique case of one truly bad writer employing another.[3]

Once he reached a certain social position, Dexter obviously felt that he should be listened to. He began to bombard the newspapers with his pronouncements and opinions. His essay on the soul, called *Wonder of Wonders*, has some intriguing ideas:

> How great the soul is! Do you not all admire and wonder to see and behold and hear? Can you all believe half the truth and admire to hear the wonders of how great the soul is! – that of a man (who) is drownded in the sea, what a great bubble comes up at the top of the water! This is wind – is the soul that is the last to ascend out of the deep to glory. The bubble is the soul.

Few men have the vision to see the soul as a huge case of cosmic wind, but Dexter's vision was, perhaps, more finely tuned.

Despite his wealth, Dexter's was not a happy life. He was married to a scolding, bad-tempered woman, father to a dissolute son, and his beloved daughter Nancy married one Abraham Bishop, described by the less-than-happy father-in-law as 'Old in Eage and larning and Coleage lant & lawyer lant and preast lant and masonik lant and Divel lant'.[4]

---

[3] Jonathan Plummer was a strange-looking man, with 'a heavy ungainly body supported by bandy legs'. He began his working life as a haddock salesman, selling the fish from a wheelbarrow. However, after a while he discovered a talent for letters – and letters of a particularly racy sort – and his wheelbarrow soon became a source of contraband pornography which he hid beneath the straw. And presumably the haddock. Perhaps this is the origin of the phrase 'there's something fishy going on here.' He took to reciting his own poems in the square, then moved into publishing, printing his own ballads and descriptions of murders and shipwrecks and the occasional sermon.

[4] 'Lant' means 'learnt'. As for the rest, you're on your own.

He also craved the respect which he thought due to him. Faced with opposition in Newburyport, he moved to Chester in New Hampshire and it was here that he first assumed the title 'Lord' Timothy Dexter, King of Chester. Perhaps it was intended as mockery, perhaps as an image of his wealth and position, but Dexter took it seriously. As he described himself in *A Pickle for the Knowing Ones*:

> Ime the first Lord in the younited States of A mercay Now of Newburyport it is the voise of the peopel and I cant Help it and so let it goue ... the first Lord in Americake the first Lord Dexter made by the voice of hamsher state my brave fellows Affirmed it they gave me the titel...

Eventually he returned to Newburyport after being physically assaulted by a lawyer who didn't like the way Timothy was flirting with his girlfriend. He purchased another stately mansion, and if many of the population viewed his return with apathy, then at least Jonathan Plummer was happy, welcoming him back with an ode:

> The town of Chester to a Lord
> Must seem a desert dull and foggy,
> A gloomy place – upon my word
> I think it dirty, wet, and boggy.
> Far different from your Kingly seat,
> In good saint James his famous street.

Dexter, apparently, lived in St James Street. Jonathan was not slow in coming forward with requests for finance:

> But I a suit of clothes must have
> To sing my joy in, and the best, sir;
> A suit of red; not black and grave,
> Provided by the earl of Chester.
> To Todd the tailor send, I pray: –
> Your Lordship's poet must be gay.

He even makes a reference to the recent unfortunate events:

You in this place have many friends,
And all the lawyers here are civil:
They know full well that envy tends
To send its owners to the devil.
I think they will not beat you blind,
Because the Nymphs to you are kind.*

*Because the Nymphs &c. – It is strongly suspected that Lord Dexter was bruised half to death, by a lawyer in New Hampshire, partly on account of the ladies' regard for him in that state. [Plummer's footnote]

Plummer received his reward. For a small stipend he became Lord Dexter's poet, decked out in a suit which, according to one report, consisted of a long black frock coat 'with stars on the corner and also on the front corners'. It also had tassels and 'fringes' and 'the whole effect was enhanced by shoes with large buckles, a large cocked hat and a gold-headed cane'. [5]

Dexter even 'crowned' his Laureate, but unable to find laurel or even mistletoe in the garden, he compromised with parsley, thus making Jonathan Plummer the world's first Poet Parsleyate.

Dexter was a true eccentric. He ornamented his house with minarets and a cupola and also his own tomb, which was surmounted by a Temple of Reason 'twelve feet suare, elevn feet high, with a hndred and fifty-eight squares of glass in it'.

He even held his funeral in advance, a kind of dress rehearsal, which most of the town attended and which became a public holiday. According to Dexter the occasion was 'tinged with gloom' and 'very much criing'. After the funeral, the mourners repaired to the house to partake of

---

[5] Plummer may have had second thoughts about the suit – he dreamt that 'wearing fringes was a sin' and tried to persuade Dexter to leave them off. Dexter refused. The moral is: be careful what you want, you might get what you thought you wanted.

refreshments – an event slightly marred by the noise of
Dexter beating his wife because she had not cried enough.

Eventually he decided that his house should become
a museum, filled with delicately carved figures. As he
described it:

> The 3 presidents, Doctor franklin John hen Cock and Mr. hamelton and
> Rouffous King and John Jea – 2 grenaders on the top of the hous, 4 lions
> below, 1 Eagle is on the Coupulow, one Lamb to lay down with one of
> the Lions – one younecorne, one Dogg, Addam and Eave in the Garden
> – one horse. The houll is not concluded as yet – Dexter's Mouseum.

He was also to add Lord Nelson, George III, Napoleon
Bonaparte and various kings of Europe, as well as the 'grand
signior of Constantinople'. On a pedestal near the road he set
up a statue of himself with the phrase 'I am first in the East'
carved under it.

In 1802 Dexter finally published his masterwork, *A Pickle
for the Knowing Ones, or Plain Truths in a Homespun Dress*. The
Newburyport Herald called it 'A thing', unable to classify it
any further. In it Dexter's orthography and syntax, which the
judicious newspaper editors normally corrected, were left
exactly as he wrote them. The *Pickle* is one of the strangest
books ever written. There is virtually no punctuation, no
sense of an overall plan, and capital letters are scattered
indiscriminately. It consists of random scenes from his life,
the plans for his museum, his views on original sin, some
thoughts on Newburyport town planning, a history of his
trading adventures, two original stories and a narrative of
the attack by the lawyer in Chester.

And in answer to those who complained about the lack of
punctuation, he had the printer put a page of full stops, com-
mas, semicolons, dashes and exclamation marks at the back
of the book, explaining that because 'the Nowing ones cam-
plane of my book the fust edition had no stops I put in A nuf
here and thay may peper and solt it as they plese'.

It is hardly what you might call 'deep'. Here is a typical
insight:

> I guess the world is one very large living creature, and always was
> and always will be without any end from everlasting to everlasting,
> and no end. What grows on this large creature is trees and many
> other things.

In one particularly significant passage, Dexter announces the
demise of the devil and the pope and proposes himself for
emperor:

> I say the grate mister Divel, that has so many Nick Names, a frind to
> the preasts, Now is dead, all, and the pope likewise, and the founders
> of mesonic, a Cheat foull of gratness of hell, Dead – preasts Dead and
> lawyers Damede Dead – A brham b Dead, and all the frined of
> mankind sing prasses that we are the grat family of mankind, Now
> out of hell Delivered from fire and smoak, mourning for Ever. Now all
> in heaven, uppon Earth, Now all frinds, Now for a day of Regoising
> all over the world, as the grate family, all Nasions, to be younited –
> No more wars for fifty years and Longer. I Recommend pease – a
> Congress in france – and when wee are Ripe for an Emper in this
> Countrey Call for me to take the helm, or a Consler in the afare or
> trouth. Amen and amen.

In his later years he was dogged by infirmity and increasing
eccentricity. [6] He even went to jail when he shot at someone
who, he thought, was 'staring' at his house.

'Lord' Timothy Dexter was larger than life. He loved to
show off. He yearned for respect but always went about
achieving it in ridiculous ways. He deserves his place in our
canon on the basis of his appalling spelling, complete lack
of punctuation and significant self-delusion. And if all that
were not enough, as he wrote once, 'Nomatter what Dexter
Rits It Dus to make the Laydes Laf at the tea tabel.'

---

[6] Hard to believe he could get any weirder, but he did.

Bibliography

Lord Timothy Dexter of Newburyport Mass., J.P. Marquand, London, 1926. It includes the full text of *A Pickle for the Knowing Ones*.

☞ Made-Up Words and Strange Syntax

Leopold John Manners De Michele; Théophile Marzials; Pedro Carolino; Nancy Luce; Amanda McKittrick Ros

☞ Philosophy and Theology

Margaret Cavendish; The Devout Salutationist; Eliza Cook; Thomas Wirgman; William Nathan Stedman; Keith Odo Newman

***

Solyman Brown (1790–1876)
Dentist and Poet

When Solyman Brown turned to poetry he obviously heeded the advice given to most authors: 'Write about what you know.' Unfortunately, in Solyman's case this meant teeth.

Dentists are frightening enough, but dentists who write poetry are utterly terrifying. Solyman was the owner of a dental supply store in Connecticut, as well as a founder of the American Society of Dental Surgeons and a partner in the wonderfully exciting New York Teeth Manufacturing Company.

So, when he turned to poetry, it was hardly surprising that he chose dentistry as his subject. His masterwork is *The Dentologia – A Poem on the Diseases of the Teeth*, a five-part celebration of all things orthodontic. One can imagine him sitting at his desk after a hard day fighting plaque, or devising a new way of manufacturing molars; he reaches for his pen, inspiration strikes and he ventures into pioneer territory – using poetry to warn people of the perils lurking in their mouths.

The Dentologia, which is subtitled *A Poem on the Diseases of the Teeth and their Proper Remedies with Notes, Practical, Historical, Illustrative and Explanatory*, runs for some fifty-four pages. There may be some people who think that the topic of dental hygiene is not particularly exciting. But Solyman overcomes this image problem with a series of dramatic vignettes.

Consider, for example, the terror of an amorous lover when his girlfriend first smiles at him:

> ... her lips disclosed to view,
> Those ruined arches, veiled in ebon hue,
> Where love had thought to feast the ravished sight
> On orient gems reflecting snowy light,
> Hope, disappointed, silently retired,
> Disgust triumphant came, and love expired!

A timely warning for all adolescents there: men do not fall in love with women who have black teeth. Or even those 'veiled in ebon hue' as Solyman prefers to put it. And, whilst there are many moments when 'disgust triumphant comes' as it were, the poem is also packed with sage advice about the preventative care of your 'orient gems':

> Whene'er along the ivory disks are seen,
> The filthy footsteps of the dark gangrene;
> When caries come,[1] with stealthy pace to throw
> Corrosive ink spots on those banks of snow,
> Brook no delay, ye trembling, suffering fair,
> But fly for refuge to the dentist's chair.

The Dentologia is one of those poems which, appropriately for a dentist, never fails to touch a nerve. Indeed, reading it is the poetic equivalent of root canal work without anaesthetic.

Originally, extracts from the poem were published in the American Journal of Dental Science, where the reviewer mystifyingly praised the author's 'rich poetic fancy' whilst being more obviously impressed by his fine grip on the science of dentistry. It is clear, indeed, that his fellow practitioners applauded Solyman's efforts. When the poem was published in book form in 1833, it came complete with a list of three hundred fellow dentists throughout the United States who had subscribed to the original molaresque work.

After the success of The Dentologia, Solyman was inspired to write a sequel, Dental Hygeia – A Poem, before expanding

---

[1] Given the reference to 'ink spots', I originally thought that 'caries' refers to the time-honoured practice of chewing one's pen. However, the word means 'decay of the bones or teeth'. You see? A poem both beautiful and informative.

his horizons into other areas of medicine with a work entitled *Cholera King*.

He was also the author of a number of pamphlets dating from the early 1800s. *A Second Address to the People of Litchfield County, New-haven 1818* is a spirited defence of himself against a charge of 'levity of character' and the removal of his licence to preach. *A Union of extremes: a discourse on liberty and slavery, as they stand related to the justice, prosperity, and perpetuity of the united republic of North America* shows that he was concerned with the key political events of his day, even if he wasn't devoted to short titles. There is also advertised *An Essay on American Poetry with Several Miscellaneous Pieces on a Variety of Subjects, Sentimental, Descriptive, Moral and Patriotic.* I have not been able to track down this exciting early work yet, although the promise of more poetry by Solyman is mouth-watering.

The Dentologia remains his triumph. Like his teeth, it will never be capped. In the admittedly limited field of dental literature, it reigns supreme. After all, many poems make you smile. But only Solyman's inspires you to brush your teeth.

Unaccountably, the poem is credited with actually raising the status of the dental profession in America. One struggles to see how, unless it proved that, compared to Solyman, normal dentists were positively well balanced.

Bibliography

The Dentologia – A Poem on the Diseases of the Teeth and their Proper Remedies with Notes, Practical, Historical, Illustrative and Explanatory, New York, 1833
Dental Hygeia – A Poem, New York, 1838
Cholera King, New York, 1842

☞ Unusual Subjects

Margaret Cavendish; Rev. Samuel Wesley; The Devout Salutationist; James Grainger; Rev. Cornelius Whur; James McIntyre; Francis Saltus Saltus; Nancy Luce

**

Reverend Cornelius Whur (1782–1853)

The Mundane Poet

The Reverend Cornelius Whur was one of those individuals who saw significance in everything. In his skilled hands, the slightest incident proved fertile ground for a poem. And for Whur every poem required a long explanation. Here, for example, is his introduction to his poem 'The Shabby Hat':

> The following lines were written at the request of a gentleman who went a journey in a rather dashing equipage, without being aware of having on a hat which ill accorded with the splendid character of his vehicle.

After such a build-up the opening lines, it must be admitted, are slightly disappointing.

> As I have nothing to be at,
> I''ll sing about the shabby hat,
> Which in some way usurped the place
> Of better one, and marred thy face.

Nothing is too small an incident to escape poetic immortality. 'The Prolific Apple Tree', for example, begins with the following preamble:

> Several years ago, a gentleman had occasion to visit a respectable family, and during tea, the lady of the establishment adverted to a remarkable apple tree which was growing in the garden; and although it was only about two feet in height, had upon it such an abundant crop of apples, as to require divers props and bandages to preserve it from injury. Tea being ended, the whole party repaired to the garden to examine the novelty...

I'll bet those long Norfolk evenings just flew by. Even then he hasn't finished describing the event, for the introduction goes on for another two hundred words or so. Finally we get to the poem, which starts well ('"See how they hang!" the lady said') but tails off rapidly.

Little is known of the good Reverend. The frontispiece of *Village Musings* shows a rather rustic-looking man, with a big nose and mutton-chop whiskers, and he appears to have followed an uneventful career as a market gardener with an even more uneventful career in the Church of England

His life may have been dull but his poems are full of surprises and delights. The titles are marvellous. He wrote poems on 'Mental Imbecility', 'The Defective Ears', 'The Cat's Dessert', 'The Thresher's Testamentary Arrangements', 'The Withered Lady' and 'The Awful Cloud' (which celebrates the untimely demise of an 'amiable gentleman, who had but just retired from the family circle, was immersed, and had perished in a cistern of boiling soap'.)

'The Poet's New Year Party' shows him turning even the common cold to poetry:

> One new year's day a Party went
> To see a certain poet,
> Esteeming it a compliment,
> Although he might not know it.
> …
> By their descent and so allied,
> Their names may here be stated: –
> Old Cough *was one; and his friend* Phlegm
> *Went too with* Short Breath, *wheezing;*
> *And old* Pain *also went with them*
> *Whom none consider pleasing!*

It is no easy task to get the word 'phlegm' into a poem with dignity, but Cornelius carries it off in his usual quiet way. Indeed, disease and infirmity were his bread and butter. Take the moving poem 'The Diseased Legs':

While they, though not of first-rate trim,
For forty years supported him:
Yet, like the changing scenes of earth,
They sometimes seemed of little worth;
And did annoy him, as would schism,
By sad complaint, called rheumatism…

Those of us whose legs have long ago ceased to be any sort of trim, let alone first rate, can empathize with these verses.

'The Unfortunate Gentleman' tells the story of a walking stick, or rather its previous owner. It begins with the lines

He whose warm hand had often pressed
Thy smoothly rounded head…

Which come as a surprise until the reader realizes that the 'you' in these verses is the walking stick, and not some small, bald person who was habitually pressed by the unfortunate gentleman. The poem has a tragic tale to tell of a man who 'upon a certain occasion gathered what he supposed to be mushrooms, in eating which himself, a sister and a little boy were poisoned'. The death is told with stark and moving power:

But in a dark and trying hour
  (Man hath his days of woe!)
He found in vegetable power
  A dreadful, deadly foe!

Although his verses abound with sudden deaths and over-whelming disability ('Be not surprised at my alarms,/ The dearest boy is without arms!') he is at his best when talking about very ordinary things as if they were world-shattering events. Here is an extract from 'The Unexpected Party':

In a most extraordinary manner about a dozen toads found their way under a hard pavement, into a kind of recess opposite a gentleman's kitchen window in a town in Suffolk.

> *A dozen hopping toads, or more,*
>   *Set out, nor aught did hinder*
> *Their progress, till they were before*
>   *A spacious kitchen window.*

The delightful rhyme of 'window' and 'hinder' hints, perhaps, at a cockney background for the Reverend.

The reader will have gathered by now that the word
'interesting' seems to have a different meaning for Cornelius.
As well as a moving lament entitled 'On The Death of an
Interesting Boy, Nine Months Old', we also have poems entitled 'The Interesting Family' and 'The Interesting Son':

> *Nor could you sigh when he was near,*
>   *Who'd your affections won,*
> *Since he was, through each rolling year,*
>   *Your interesting son.*

Nowhere, however, does he explain to the reader what was
interesting about these people. Rev. Whur, it seems, had a
totally different idea about what was interesting than the rest
of the world.

His most famous poem is 'The Female Friend', wherein he
sings the joys of feminine company:

> *Will not a beauteous landscape bright,*
>   *Or music's soothing sound,*
> *Console the heart, afford delight*
>   *And throw sweet peace around?*
> *They may, but never comfort lend*
> *Like an accomplish'd female friend!*

The title always reminds me of the Roy Rogers song 'A Four
Legged Friend', but whereas Roy was singing about a horse,
at least the Rev. Whur has someone to make him a cup of tea
and listen to his 'exciting' stories:

The fragrance of the blushing rose,
  Its tints and splendid hue
Will with the season decompose
  And pass as flitting dew;
On firmer ties his joys depend
Who has a polish'd female friend!

And that is how I like to imagine him. Sitting quietly in the fading evening light, in the drawing room of his Norfolk rectory, thoughtfully polishing his female friend with a damp cloth.

Bibliography

Village Musings on Moral and Religious Subjects, Norwich, 1837
Gratitude's Offering, being Original Productions on a Variety of Subjects, Norwich, 1845

☞ Unusual Subjects
Margaret Cavendish; Rev. Samuel Wesley; The Devout Salutationist; James Grainger; James McIntyre; Solyman Brown; Francis Saltus Saltus; Nancy Luce

Hymns Ancient and Appalling

For the collectors of truly bad literature, hymn writing has a high place. Probably because of the sheer numbers of hymns that have been churned out over the centuries, there are many pleasingly bad examples.

Frequently man is likened to a worm, with surprising results. First we have a talking worm:

> *Earth from afar has heard Thy fame,*
> *And worms have learnt to lisp thy name.*
> Hymnodist unknown

Then we have an invading worm:

> *O may thy powerful word*
> *Inspire the feeble worm*
> *To rush into thy kingdom, Lord,*
> *And take it as by storm.*
> The Wesleyan Hymnbook

And finally we have a retired worm:

> *In age and feebleness extreme,*
> *Who shall a helpless worm redeem?*
> Charles Wesley

It's not just the worms who get involved. An unknown American hymn writer wrote:

> *Ye monsters of the bubbling deep*
> *Your maker's praises shout;*
> *Up from the sand, ye codlings leap*
> *And wag your tails about.*

Which was echoed by Isaac Watts:

> *Amidst Thy watery kingdoms, Lord,*
>   *The finny nations play,*
> *And scaly monsters at Thy word*
>   *Rush through the northern sea.*

I'm not quite sure what he means by 'finny nations' here. Possibly Finland.

Religious poetry is also good for a laugh. Richard Crashaw depicted Mary Magdalene following Jesus about like a sort of mobile drinks machine:

> *And now where'er He strays,*
> *Among the Galilean mountains,*
> *Or more unwelcome ways,*
> *He's followed by two faithful fountains;*
> *Two walking baths; two weeping motions;*
> *Portable and compendious oceans...*

He means that she is crying. Isaac Watts used a similar image in one of his poems:

> *Hark! she bids all her friends adieu;*
> *Some angel calls her to the spheres;*
> *Our eyes the radiant saint pursue*
> *Through liquid telescopes of tears.*
> from 'On the Sudden Death of Mrs. Mary Peacock'

In fact, Watts was greatly into crying:

> *Come Saints and drop a tear or two*
> *On the dear bosom of your God.*

Bible history is very popular. Here are the reflections of a couple of unknown authors.

So Samson, when his hair was lost,
Met the Philistines to his cost,
Shook his huge limbs with vain surprise,
Made feeble flight, and lost his eyes.

By whom shall Jacob now arise?
  For Jacob's friends are few;
And what may fill us with surprise,
  They seem divided too.

The real fun happens when words change their meanings. I recall singing as a young boy in church the words 'Here I raise my Ebenezer', without anyone explaining to me that it meant 'memorial stone'. A Methodist hymn seems to imply that the angels are getting a bit above themselves:

Jesus faithful to His word,
  Shall with a shout descend;
All heaven's host their glorious Lord
  Shall pompously attend.

Pompously in this sense meant 'with pomp and ceremony'. Bowels have changed as well, if you'll pardon the expression. In early times bowels meant 'inmost being', rather than the more intestinal definition we give them today. Thus we have Charles Wesley writing:

> *My stony heart Thy voice shall rent,*
>   *Thou wilt, I trust, the veil remove;*
> *My inmost bowels shall resent*
>   *The yearnings of Thy dying love.*

Not that the bowel confusion removes the difficulties with this verse. Is his stony heart being rented by God's voice? And why should his bowels resent some yearnings? But resent in the eighteenth century meant, in Dr Johnson's definition, 'to take well or ill'. And I think Wesley means his heart will be rent as in 'torn'. Another poet wrote:

> *He knows our frame, and with parental love*
> *He chides our follies while his bowels move.*
> J. Pickering, from *Pathetical and Consolatory Poems*

Sometimes the word in question is meant literally. Here Wesley means that the darts are blunt, but he makes it sound as though the whole thing is unutterably boring:

> *His love, surpassing far*
>   *The love of all beneath,*
> *We find within our hearts, and dare*
>   *The pointless darts of death.*

I leave the last word, however, to Mrs Hamilton-King, a writer whose only surviving lines tell us something remarkable about the creator:

> *God formed in the hollow of his hand*
> *This ball of Earth among His other Balls...*

Stephen Fawcett (fl. 1837)
Northern Junketing Fanatic

*F*awcett is a minor character whose reputation rests on one book: *Wharfedale Lays, Or Lyrical Poems*. The preface contains a fine defence of the bad poet:

> *Though my birth was low, my education comparatively little, my means small, my time short, my labour hard, and my literary discouragement great, yet I hold that no excuse for the production of a dull book.*

And he certainly shows a skill in rhyming. 'Verses Written in Sickness' contains one of my favourite lines:

> *The death watch is ticking by the bed that's the sick in…*

It doesn't make sense, but it sounds wonderful. The poem also contains the striking thought:

> *O who, in youth's bud thinks he ever will cling*
> *To that skeleton blanch'd in death's oozy bed?*

Few youngsters, it has to be agreed, lie in bed and think of such things.[1] Elsewhere, however, Fawcett's natural breeziness bursts out. He is very keen on 'junketting'. Everyone 'junkets' in Fawcett's work, even medieval knights and squires:

> *But the minstrel is heard, and there's junketting now…*
> …
> *An archer awaited – his merry horn blew,*
> *The bridge rattled down to give way,*

---

[1] Apart from art students.

The ban-dog howl'd loud as the gates open flew,
And a dim fearful twilight the massive arch knew,
That he pass'd to the junketting gay.

I don't know who has passed to the gay junket, but it could be the dog.

Like all bad poets, he was not above inventing words if he could not find exactly the right term. 'The Sun Rising' contains an intriguing new word to describe the sun's journey:

On surges huge of living fire
His chariot wheels are borne;
And, on his skyey journey bent,
He bursts the gates of morn.

And one remembers, with joy, the romantic question

What has he whisper'd in Beauty's lug?

It is a pity that Stephen didn't write more. Anyone capable of writing a line like that obviously has talent. Perhaps he was just too busy junketting.

Bibliography

Wharfedale Lays, Or Lyrical Poems, London & Bradford, 1837

☞ Minor Victorians
Eliza Cook; Leopold John Manners De Michele; Alfred Austin; J. Stanyan Bigg; Pownoll Toker Williams

***

Thomas Baker (fl. 1837–57)
Poet, Engineer, Train Spotter

Thomas Baker is the Poet Laureate of the trainspotting fraternity, an original poet whose reputation rests on just one poem: *The Steam Engine; or, the Powers of Flame, an Original Poem in Ten Cantos.*

Although in the book he is merely called T. Baker, the British Library identifies him as Thomas Baker, author of several volumes on civil engineering. On the qualities of these it is difficult to comment, for works like *Railway Engineering, Treatise on the Mathematical Theory of the Steam Engine* and *The Elements of Practical Mechanism and Machine Tools (With remarks on tools and machinery by James Nasmyth)* do not hold out a lot of promise of entertainment.[1]

However, his poetry is a different matter. In around two hundred pages of thrilling verse, *The Steam Engine* takes us on a whirlwind ride through the history of steam power. The preface, dated 25 April 1857, gives us a hint of the excitement to come:

> *It will be evident from a perusal of the poem, even to one who has never previously turned much of his attention to the development of the Steam-Powers, that they have deeply impressed themselves upon the inventive intellect of a very high order of men...*

In other words, it will be more interesting than we think. Alas, the early pages of the poem do not bear this out, and only

---

[1] I did have hopes of *A Rudimentary Treatise on Mensuration, comprehending the elements of modern engineering,* London, 1850, but it turns out that mensuration means measuring lines, volumes and solids, so I haven't bothered.

Thomas's most ardent fans would avoid skipping the medieval chapters. It is not until we hit Canto IV that things really start to move, with the invention of the paddle boat and the web-footed genius of Lord Stanhope:

> Lord Stanhope hit upon a novel plan
> Of bringing forth this vast Leviathan
> (This notion first Genevois' genius struck);
> His frame was made to emulate the duck;
> Webb'd feet had he, in Ocean's brine to play;
> With whale like might, he whirl'd aloft the spray;
> But made with all this splash but little speed;
> Alas the duck was doom'd not to succeed!
>
> Canto IV, Part xii

As other editors have pointed out, a hasty reading of this verse seems to imply that Lord Stanhope was built like a duck, albeit a duck with 'whale like might'.[2] However, closer inspection reveals that the author is talking about a paddle-steamer. Of course, Lord Stanhope may have resembled a duck or a whale. Or both. It may be an ironic masterstroke. Or it may simply be bad punctuation.

In Canto VI we travel with Thomas on the Cork Packet, a steam boat travelling across the North Sea. It was not a happy journey. The sea was rough and so were some of the passengers, who, amazingly for a boat bound for Ireland, he identifies as being Irish.

> Tourists there were, and trav'llers mercantile,
> In groups too, were the sons of Erin's Isle...

These had apparently been to London and, ignoring the culture and learning, had embarked on 'what's called a spree'. Other passengers include a naval captain, and

---

[2] Moby Duck, perhaps.

> *an Irish squire an agriculturist,*
> *Whose name, too, figured on the Epsom list,*
> *whom afterwards I often met elsewhere,*
> *with me most blandly made acquaintance there.*
> ...
> *But few at table had as yet quite done,*
> *Save those whom sickness had compell'd to run;*
> *When lo, the wind grew strong and veer'd around,*
> *The vessel pitch'd, the waves began to bound,*
> *With louder creaking of both cord and mast,*
> *Which put at once an end to the repast;*
> *Except the tailor not yet satisfied,*
> *Who still voracious, at the viands plied!*
> *High pitch'd the car, the sea began to roar;*
> *The tailor, careless still, eat more and more!*
> *But dire sea-sickness, all unwelcome came,*
> *With sudden pounce upon his well-gorged frame;*
> *The table, carpet, crimson-cover'd bench,*
> *Received at once a most unsightly drench!*
> ...
> *A squall came next, aloft th' vessels pitch'd,*
> *The ladies squall'd too, and with sickness retch'd.*
> Canto VI, Part vi

After all this throwing up it is a relief to get back to the steam engines. Canto VII tends to get a little detailed for my liking:

> *But paucton's snake-like screw, behind the car,*
> *The best propellor for the CHIEFS OF WAR,*
> *Is safely placed beneath the rolling sea,*
> *And thus preserved from scaith of gun-shot free.*
> *Rennie's conoidal triple-bladed screw*
> *Displaced the last...*
> Canto VII, Part xi

But he does have some fine rhymes slipped in there:

> Lo a physician greater still than all,
> With added proofs of skill came forth, 'twas Hall!
>
> Canto VII, Part x

He scores a similar triumph at the end of the book:

> The TUBULAR VIADUCT, so ably plann'd,
> In iron's strength, he arms of ocean spann'd;
> The grand design of Junior Stephenson,
> No nobler work by him was ever done.
>
> Canto X, Part x

I don't know if George Stephenson ever called his son Junior – it sounds a bit American to me. Mind you, strange things happen to a man when he climbs up on to the footplate. For by now we are into the age of railways and Thomas's full powers are 'steaming ahead', especially in his description of the death of Huskisson, the first man to be run over by a railway train:

> The trains are stopp'd, the MIGHTY CHIEFS OF FLAME
> To quench their thirst the crystal water claim;
> While from their post the great in crowds alight,
> When, by a line-train, in its hasty flight,
> Though striving to avoid it, Huskisson
> By unforeseen mischance was over-run.
>
> Canto X, Part iii

It is a curious fact that, in one of the London parks, Huskisson is commemorated with a statue in which he is, unaccountably, dressed in a toga. Of course, he may have been wearing the toga at the time, which would account for the reason he had difficulty getting out of the way. However, his death cast something of a pall over the day:

> The fatal chance not only caused delay,
> But damped the joy that erst had crown'd the day.
>
> Canto X, Part x

Baker's outlook on life may be summed up in a phrase from his poem:

> *What can't Steam and gold united do?*

At times, he is so struck with awe as to be transported into a positively numinous state:

> *Their god-like prowess, and their length of car,*
> *Made gazers all, with great reluctance, see*
> *Their own comparative nonentity.*
> Canto VII, Part ii

Maybe I have been wrong all these years. Maybe trainspotters are not merely noting down numbers and gauges and times, but undergoing an experience of numinous intensity, and comprehending anew their insignificance in the great scheme of things.

Or maybe they are just sad people in kagouls.

Bibliography

The Steam Engine; or, the Powers of Flame, an Original Poem in Ten Cantos, London, 1857

☞ Boats and Trains
Reverend Edward Dalton; Frederick James Johnston-Smith; *Titanic* Poets

Pedro Carolino a.k.a. José da Fonseca (1788–1866)

The Worst Ever Linguist

It is difficult to know which name to give to this giant among bad writers. In the catalogue of the Bodleian Library he is listed as José da Fonseca, but on the title page of his book he gives his name as Pedro Carolino.

Whichever is correct, he will go down in history as the worst translator ever. His reputation rests on one book – *The New Guide Of The Conversation In Portuguese And English*.

The book purports to be a phrasebook and dictionary of the English language for Portuguese students, but a glance at some of the phrases shows at once that this is no ordinary guide. Among the useful English phrases are 'Assure hi from mi remembrance', 'have you say that?' and 'These apricots and these peaches make me and to come water in my mouth.'

The author provides the names of English food such as 'Some wigs',[1] 'A chitterling sausages', and 'An amelet'. And there are many dialogues to show English in action:

Dialogue 16
For to see the town

Anthony, go to accompany they gentilsmen, do they see the town.
We won't to see all that is remarquable here.
Come with me, if you please. I shall not folget nothing what can to merit your attention. Here we are near to cathedral; will you come in there?
We will first to see him in oudside, after we shall go in there for to look the interior.

---

[1] Eggs. Probably.

> *Admire this master piece gothic architecture's.*
> The chasing of all they figures is astonishing indeed.

The problem with the book is that Pedro, apparently, didn't actually *know* any English. Instead, he used a Portuguese–French phrasebook and then a French–English dictionary. His introduction gives a clear idea of what to expect:

> *we did put, with a scrupulous exactness, a great variety own expressions to english and portuguese idioms; without to attach us selves (as make some others) almost at a literal translation; translation what only will be for to accustom the portuguese pupils, or-foreign, to speak very bad any of the mentioned idioms.*

I hope that's all clear, then. Pedro goes on to speak of his hopes for his little book:

> *We expect then, who the little book (for the care what we wrote him, and for her typographical correction) that may be worth the acceptation of the studious persons, and especially of the Youth, at which we dedicate him particularly.*

The book is split into several sections. The first part gives a long list of useful terms. In the section entitled 'Of The Man' various parts of the body are given, such as:

> *The fat of the leg*
> *The brain*
> *The brains.*
> *The superior lip*
> *The inferior lip*
> *The prepuce*

Under 'degrees of kindred' we find:

> *The bastard woman*
> *The bastard man*
> *The gosip mistress*
> *A cousin*
> *An cousin*
> *The quater-grandfather*
> *The quater-grandmother*

The book provides not only the English 'equivalent' but a phonetic guide to pronunciation. Under 'Eatings', Carolino gives us

Some black pudding	Seume blak pud'din-gue
Some wigs	Seume uiges
A chitterling sausages	E txitt'–eur-lin-ne sasedje
An amelet	An ame'–lett
A little mine	E lit'–tl-maine
Vegetables boiled to a pap	Vejetabls boiled tu e pap

'Drinkings' includes

Some liquors	Seume lik'eurs
Some orgeat	Seume or-djá-te
Some paltry wine	Seume pal-try uai-ne

After these simple terms, Carolino moves on to familiar phrases, such as

Bring me a knife.
Go to send for.
Have you something to command to.
Assure hi from mi remembrance.
have you say that?
have you understand that he says?
At what is employed that?
At what purpose have say so?
Apply you at the study during that you are young.
Dress your hairs.

A little further on, things start to get nasty and the visitor's useful phrases include:

he has pull me the book by hands.
he laughs at my nose, he jest by me.
He has spit in my coat.
He has me take out my hairs.
He does me some kicks.
he make them on purpose.

i am confused all yours civilities.
You interompt me.
You mistake your self heavily.

In the second section of the book, the student is given some dialogues and it is here that Pedro really comes into his own. Dialogue 1 starts with a few basics:

Good morning sir, how do you do today?
Very well I thank you.
To much oblige to you.
I am very glad and to see you in a good health.
I am ready at your service.
I thank you.
How does your father do?
Very well.

Dialogue 2 is entitled 'For to make a visit in the morning':

Is your master at home?
Yes, sir.
Is it up?
No sir, he sleep yet.

The dialogues are studded with absolute gems. Dialogue 13, 'For to buy', would come in handy to anyone negotiating with their tailor:

What will you have, sir.
I won't have a good and fine cloth to make a coat.
Come in sir, you shall see here the best cloth of Paris.
Show me the best what you have.
Here it is a much fine and who bear now.
...
How much do you sell it the ell?[2]
We thout overcharge you from a halfpenny, it cost twenty franks.
Sir, I am not accustomed to cheapen; tell me the last price.

---

[2] 'Ell' is an archaic measure of length. He is not asking 'how the 'ell do you sell this?'

I have told you, sir, it is valuable in that.
It is much too dear, I give at it, eighteen franks.
There is not one halfpenny to beat down.

…

I want some casimire for to make me a pair of pantaloons.
Here is i bysides what shall please you too much, it is what there is in last fashion.

There are some forty-three dialogues, including 'With a Joweller' (37), 'For Embarking One's self' (29) and 'To Inform One'self of a person' (17). Dialogue 43 has a certain interest, given the genesis of the book:

Dialogue 43
The French Language

Do you study?
Yes, sir, I attempts to translate of french by portuguese.
The you learn the french language? You do well the french language becomes us all days too much necessary. What books have you there?
It is a grammar and a vocabulary.
Do you know already the principal grammars rules?
I am apleed my self at to learn its by heart.

…

Do you speak french alwais?
Some times; though I flay it yet.
You jest, you does express you self very well.

And from Dialogue 4, 'The Walk', comes this charming vignette of rural life:

You hear the bird's gurgling.
With pleasure! which charm!

There then follows a section of 'familiar letters' from famous people such as Boileau, Racine and Madame de Sévigné, revealing some curious inadequacies in their prose style. Racine, the great French playwright, writes:

> My uncle what will to treat her beshop in a great sumptuousness, he
> was go to Avignon for to buy what one not should find there...

It is a perplexing letter and I am surprised at Racine for not
writing with more precision. Is the uncle, or the bishop a
'she'? And what will one not find at Avignon that is such a
sumptuous treat? Meanwhile, from Madame de Sévigné we
get

> Madame Of Sevigné at their daughter
> I write you every day: it is a jay which give me most favourable at all
> who beg me some letters.

While the philosopher Rousseau reveals an unexpectedly
muddled piece of thinking:

> With a single friend as you, sir, should be one's self always quiet, if
> the acknowledgement was exclude the confusion. The mine grow to
> the sight of yours kindnesses.

Section four is a fascinating selection of anecdotes. Probably
the best is the extremely moving death of the Duke of
Northumberland:

> As he felt to approach her last hour he was commanded to hers
> servants to arm of all parts, and they were put him upon a armchair,
> keeping the bare-sword. He was challenged the death as a blusterer.

And for those of a more classical turn of mind, we are transported back to Ancient Greece:

> The sophist Zenon, the most hardy of all men at to sustain some para-
> doxes, was denied one day, before Diogenes, the existence of the
> motion. This was put him self immediately to make two or three turns
> in the session-house.[3]

Finally there is the section called, with stunning appropriate-
ness, 'Idiotisms and Proverbs'. This includes a superb list of

---

[3] I don't blame him. If you are denied the existence of a motion, then the
only thing is to spend an hour or two in the session-house.

English proverbs – many of which sound vaguely familiar, but with an exotic twist:

> *The necessity don't know the low.*
> *To meet any-one nose at nose.*
> *What come in to me for an ear yet out for another.*
> *There is not any ruler without a exception.*

Then there are the frankly weird:

> *He has the throat paved.*
> *Nothing some money, nothing of Swiss.*
> *To buy a cat in pocket.*
> *To craunch the marmoset.*
> *To come back at their muttons.*

The book was so funny that many claimed it was a deliberate parody. Mark Twain in his introduction to the 1884 edition pointed out the difficulty of faking it this well:

> *It was written in serious good faith and deep earnestness, by an honest and upright idiot, who believed he knew something of the English language, and could impart his knowledge to others… There are sentences in this book which could have been manufactured by a man in his right mind, and with an intelligent and deliberate purpose to seem innocently ignorant; but there are other sentences and paragraphs which no mere pretended ignorance could ever achieve.*

Twain cites as evidence the author's belief that as with most European languages,

> *the indefinite article has a sex. He thinks a is masculine and an feminine … it would not occur to anybody to invent this blunder, but it is a blunder which an ignorant foreigner would quite naturally fall into.*

The New Guide Of The Conversation In Portuguese And English is the work of a truly great translator – a translator who was so confident of his ability that he didn't bother to translate the words into a language he actually knew. Mark Twain, in a passage which applies to all the greatest awful literature, writes:

Whatsoever is perfect in its kind in literature, is imperishable: nobody can add to the absurdity of this book, nobody can imitate it successfully, nobody can hope to produce its fellow; it is perfect, it must and will stand alone: its immortality is secure.

Bibliography

A New Guide of the Conversation In Portuguese and English, London, 1884

☞ Four Stars and Better
Margaret Cavendish; James McIntyre; Joseph Gwyer; Julia Moore; William MacGonagall; Francis Saltus Saltus; Théophile Marzials; Walter Reynolds; Shepherd M. Dugger; Amanda McKittrick Ros

☞ Made-Up Words and Strange Syntax
'Lord' Timothy Dexter; Leopold John Manners De Michele; Théophile Marzials; Nancy Luce; Amanda McKittrick Ros

☞ Tales of Travel
Bloodgood H. Cutter; Thomas Costley; Shepherd M. Dugger; Frederick James Johnston-Smith

***

Reverend William Cook (1807?–76)

The William Blake of Bad Poetry[1]

William Cook was a renaissance man. Author, illustrator, printer and even binder, he produced over forty pamphlets of some of the most wonderfully execrable poetry ever. He had his own printing press, engraved his own woodblocks and even did some pioneering work in crayon. Like William Blake he was poet, artist and visionary. Unlike William Blake he was bad at all three.

An ordained minister, he lived in Salem, Massachusetts, where, despite his eccentricities, he was a successful teacher of mathematics and book-keeping. However, no prophet is entirely without persecution, and one dark day, a small chapel which he had erected on a hilltop was burned down. It immediately drew a poetic response:

While at home I preached this doctrine
Without any consent of mine
A being in destruction arch
Went to my bethel with a torch.

Of his literary style he says proudly, 'My rhythm is original and varied to please my taste', a statement borne out by all of his poems. Take, for example, his great work *Talk About Indians*, which includes the verse:

Corn, corn, sweet Indian corn,
*   Greenly you grew long ago.*
Indian fields well to adorn,
*   And to parch or grind hah ho!*

[1] Of course, some people would argue that William Blake should be the William Blake of bad poetry.

'Hah ho!' is a wonderful ending to the line, although it is not made clear who is hah-ing and who ho-ing.

His long poem 'Chestnut Street' contains five or six illustrations in black and white and two others in coloured crayon. One of these shows, apparently, a female martyr being led away by a soldier in a toga – which suggests that Salem in the early nineteenth century was a lot more cosmopolitan than one would imagine.

His poem 'The Ploughboy' paints a rosy picture of rural life:

> Low gable roof, and all sides brown
> > The cottage by the moor
> Has a charming site out from town,
> > And the inmates were four.

> There Jerome and Roland were born,
> > And Ellen their sister,
> Whose cradle rockers, so much worn,
> > Could be rocked no faster.

And chief, perhaps, amongst their worn-out rockers was their grandmother, who, despite her advancing years, still apparently comes in handy:

> Their grandmother useful, though old,
> > As people used to talk,
> To those children good stories told
> > At home or in a walk.

Cook was a versatile and educated man. Uniquely for a modern poet, perhaps, he had the ability to be bad in Latin as well. His poem 'Frémont', which celebrates the marriage between General Frémont and Miss Jessie Benton, begins in style:

> Nequis currit facile in sua vi,
> > Libre proinde,
> Vires dantur commodum eo rogantur;
> > Ad bona car sit,

> *Canto juvat quenque gratis canere laudes,*
> > *Itaque evax*
> *Laete pro Fremonte et Jessie suscito carmen.*

Which translates as

> *No one in self with ease makes speed,*
> > *Freely therefore*
> *Aids are fitly granted where sought;*
> > *If pious be th' heart,*
> *Song helps each one gladly to sing praises,*
> > *So said 'tis huzza*
> *Lively for Frémont and Jessie I make th' strain.*

I don't speak Latin, but then again, reading Cook's poetry gives me the impression I don't speak English either. 'Frémont' is the story of a dashing buffalo-killer and his love, and Cook brings us thrillingly close to the heart of nature:

> *Lo, yonder through the distant groves*
> *Th' raging buffaloes came*
> *Rolling dust and bellowing sound*
> *Told that they were not fondly tame,*
> *That they were not gentle as doves*
> *As dashed the hunters through the droves*
> *After game that hungry man loves,*
> *And by the fierce daring combat,*
> *Gained were sirloins, juicy and fat.*
>
> *...*
>
> *A bird was near the nestlings dear,*
> *Think my friends, if such scenes be found,*
> *That Frémont in notes did resound,*
> *That Jessie in echo did bound,*
> *Frémont though bold had a kind heart,*
> *And that bird could move it like art.*

It is not clear here whether the bird is a literal bird, or whether he is referring, in rather familiar tones, to Jessie.

William Cook is unique among the ranks of bad poets for combining bad verse with bad art to produce an impressive all-round effect. He couldn't write and he couldn't draw either – an irresistible combination.

Bibliography

Cook's works were mainly published in the form of numerous individual pamphlets. These are just some of the lowlights:

The Ploughboy, Salem, 1854
Talk About Indians, Salem, 1873
Chestnut Street, Salem, 1857
Frémont, a Poem, Salem, 1856; 1868

☞ Falero-lero-loo, Riddlety-diddlety Poets
George Wither; James Whitcomb Riley; Théophile Marzials; Rev. Edward Dalton

The Five Golden Rules of Bad Writing
2. If It Won't Rhyme, Force It

In poetry, any bad writer knows that any rhyme will do. It doesn't matter if it's a good rhyme, as long as the line endings sound roughly the same. Often, very roughly the same. All right, often, only the same if the reader pronounced them in an ridiculous way.

For example:

James McIntyre's 'Dairy Ode' begins with a barrage of truly abysmal lines:

> *When cows give milk from spring fodder*
> *You cannot make a good cheddar.*
> *The quality is often vile*
> *Of cheese that is made in April...*

And Joseph Gwyer's charming poem for his son combines appalling rhymes with nauseating cuteness:

> *I wish you Alfred now a good night;*
> *You gives your mother great delight;*
> *Don't you wake up and ask for baa,*
> *Or you'll offend your dad-dad-a.*

The poet informs us that the little Alfred calls bread 'baa', and water 'waa', a fact which explains the rhyme, but does not excuse it. One imagines that his mother would say to her son, 'If you don't behave yourself, Daddy will write you a poem.'

The Minor Victorians

J. Stanyan Bigg (fl. 1848–62)
The Furness Philosopher

Bigg, like Fawcett, was a poet of the north-west of England. He was a journalist and editor who published a series of long, intense poems. *Night and the Soul* is a lengthy verse drama which begins rather moodily:

> How deep the silence of these hoary woods,
> Unbroken by the flutter of a wing,
> Ungloom'd by not a throb of life...

After a while, the gloom lifts as along throb two young men who discuss the pointlessness of existence. One, named Alexis, says:

> It is as if, on mighty themes like this,
> Language with puny, frantic arms, strove hard
> To fold a mountain in its weak embrace.
> We seek to paint the darkness, and our brush
> Smears nothing but itself.

Needless to say, all this smearing finally gets to him and he is lost in a haze of nihilism:

> There is no good, no evil, and no law,
> No right or wrong, no Hell, no Heaven, no God,
> Nothing but thee and orderless decay!
> And her, – black, – coiling in extremest space
> A hideous doom seems whetting its grim jaws ...

To which his companion Ferdinand replies, rather breezily,

> Nightmare, my friend – and heavy suppers – hey?

Bigg is certainly capable of striking images. Here he talks about 'thought' in terms of an enormous tongue:

> *Whether it stretches up*
> *In grand cathedral spires, whose gilded vanes*
> *Like glorious earth-tongues, lap the light of heaven…*

Whilst his view of the soul is curiously reminiscent of Timothy Dexter:

> *And the soul rises into buoyancy,*
> *Balloon-like, puff'd out with the gas of gods…*

His picture of a stricken queen summons up distressing images of ladies' fashion in the early 1970s:

> *The world stood hush'd beneath the blazing sky,*
> *Like a Queen stricken in her marriage robes;*
> *One almost heard the great hot heart of noon*
> *Throb in the silence with fierce passion-pants.*[1]
> *…*
> *A solemn hush is over sea and sky*
> *Save when hot pants come sobbing through the air…*

Shifting Scenes and Other Poems is a more personal book and, mercifully, a lot shorter. 'Enemies at Court' is set in an oriental palace where two princes discuss the habits of certain local predators:

> *The tiger-cat is brave who tears our kids;*
> *The lion is no coward, though he kills*
> *And munches in the dark.*

While 'Remorse' tells us that there is something nasty lurking in the shadows:

> *And the stone stems sprout out their living buds,*
> *And all the ceiling tumble o'er with blooms*
> *In the high-mounting jubilance – and yet*

---

[1] I had a pair of fierce passion-pants once, but the elastic went.

There is a white and glimmering ghastliness
Somewhere behind the arras!

In Bigg's work, indeed, there is always the feeling that beneath the bright colours, behind the flowers and the costume, our arrases hide a hideous secret.

Like many of his contemporaries, he was never able to resist a good death. His sombre commemoration of a pit disaster portrays Death as a graffiti artist:

Death in the palace; Death within the Cot;
Death in all ranks! 'Tis but the common lot.
Death writes the fearful legend up 'No More'.
Over the mantelpiece, and on the floor.

from 'The Hartley Pit Catastrophe'

While his historical piece, 'The Huguenot's Doom', depicts a terrible family tragedy:

Oh are ye men, and have ye hearts of steel
That for no human woe can feel,
To whom love's agony is nought?
I tell you I'm the youngest son of five;
And three lie in their gore
Down by the great hall-door,
And Fred and I are all that are left alive! [2]

He also wrote a novel, *Alfred Staunton*, large chunks of which are in the local Furness dialect. I know that it starts in a coach station at Lancaster, but I must admit that, after a while, the endless local dialect is a right pain in the arras.

---

[2] And Fred's not feeling too well.

Bibliography

Night and the Soul, London, 1854
Shifting Scenes and Other Poems, London, 1862
Alfred Staunton, London, 1859

☞ Minor Victorians

Eliza Cook; Stephen Fawcett; Leopold John Manners De Michele; Alfred Austin; Pownoll Toker Williams

☞ Dialects and Accents

James Whitcomb Riley; 'Child' Poems; Amanda McKittrick Ros

James Henry Powell (b. 1830)
Poet, Lecturer, Mesmerist

I first saw the light of day in London, in the year 1830. My parents were poor, their poverty being aggravated by the glass.[1]

*S*o begins *Life Incidents and Poetic Pictures*, the thoroughly depressing autobiography and collection of verse by James Henry Powell. The book is one long collection of illness, injury, poverty, lost jobs, failed businesses and dying relatives. In the first few pages alone he falls over running for a bus, is nearly crushed by a horse, almost run down by a train and partially drowned whilst swimming. And those are the cheerful bits.

After leaving school he worked as an engineer in a bewildering number of jobs, from each of which he was dismissed or forced to retire. Sometimes he fell ill, sometimes he was sacked for his 'free-thinking' tendencies, sometimes his teetotalism made him the object of bullying. In one notable case he set up a grocer's business only to be defrauded of twenty shillings (actually fifteen shillings cash and some tea) by an unscrupulous pencil salesman. So much for chapters one and two.

Chapter three begins on a more cheerful note:

It is well we do not possess prescience… If we did there would be little exercise of hope and certainly a vast increase of suicides.

By this time the reader is beginning to feel slightly depressed. However, all is not lost. Powell, as an alternative to suicide or despair, decides to write poetry instead:

[1] He means they drank a lot. Or perhaps they had an unprofitable window-cleaning business.

As I suffered I sung, always earnest, but rarely artistic. The fact is, I knew little or nothing of the rules of versification; I sang, however, my first song and was delighted at the sound of my own voice... The idea came to me to publish a small collection of my early poetic effusions, and I was unwise enough to issue 'The Poet's Voice', a work both crude in conception and defective in execution.

Typically of Powell it didn't work. He secured about sixty subscribers, but half of them never paid.

As a poet he spoke mainly about the areas on which he was an expert: injury, sadness, depression and being run over by trains. Here, for example, are a few lines from his celebrated poem 'Lines Written to a Friend on the Death of His Brother, Caused by a Railway Train Running Over Him Whilst He Was in a State of Inebriation':

Thy mangled corpse upon the rails in frightful shape was found.
The ponderous train had killed thee as its heavy wheels went round,
And thus in dreadful form thou met'st a drunkard's awful death
And I, thy brother, mourn thy fate, and breathe a purer breath.

'The Dying Seamstress' tells a tragic tale of a needleworker on her way out:

Upon her couch of pain she beckon'd friends to her most dear,
Her thin pale hands were clasp'd in prayer, and angels hover'd near;
Dear mother, sister, Willie true; I'm dying; kiss me all;
Some other hands than mine must make the dress for Monday's ball.
...
Oh let me die, dear mother, and fear not for your child,
In Heaven I shall not hem and sew, until my brain turns wild.

And his long, autobiographical poem 'The Rustic Rhymer' has much to commend it:

Oh! There's a magic influence in Song,
To throb the soul with ecstasy divine,
And bid her soar on pinions flutt'ring strong,
Where Freedom's congregated orb-lights shine,
And Truth maintains her unpolluted shrine.

I have no idea what Freedom's congregated orb-lights are, unless they are some kind of system for lighting churches. The poem contains a fine example of elision – the omitting of a syllable to make the word scan:

> And parents and their children meet as foes,
> In Mammon's 'peting Mart where life swoons out in throes...

Bad poets are always keen on elision, as adding apostrophes makes their poetry seem, well, more *poetic*. In some of his poems, Powell even chose to remove syllables that didn't exist:

> Tho' oft depress'd, when stung by serpent Guile,
> Tho' oft made sad, by sorrows bred by Scorn;
> Mayhap to disappointment doom'd the while,

There is absolutely no difference in pronunciation between 'Though' and 'Tho'. It just *looks* so much more like a poem when a few elisions are chucked in. In spite of all his trials, he is determined to end triumphantly. Alas, the triumph is cruelly dashed. Even here, in the final stanza of his first book and the final stanza of his most personal poem he is dogged by ill-luck. Typically for the hapless Powell there is a typo:

> Inspir'd by Truth, the Rustic Bhymer sings,
> And dreams of Beauty, Fame's capricious smile,
> And eats the crust that honest Labour brings,
> More gifted, blest, than glittering hosts of conqu'ring kings.

Throughout his work, the Rustic Bhymer shows a moving compassion for those worse off than himself, although such people are difficult to find. Here is part of the poem delicately titled 'Idiot Bessie':

> The idiot maid may never feel
> Such kind and soothing care:
> Nor can she even half reveal
> The wild curious thoughts that steal
> Upon her with despair:

> For Bessie, tho' an idiot born,
> Doth feel, at times, the sting of scorn,
> That kindness fails to spare.

Unsurprisingly, perhaps, the poetry never paid its way. He eventually took up mesmerism, almost by accident. Having tried everything else, I suppose that hypnotism was the only profession he hadn't tried. Amazingly, he found himself to be quite good at it, and for the rest of his life he plied the trade of a travelling hypnotist. Even then, money was tight:

> Sometimes at the end of a week's hard and, I may add now, honest mesmerizing, I brought home enough money to support my family during the following week; at other times the battle was harder and yet the profits smaller.

One can imagine him arriving home, tired and cross-eyed after having to stare at a gently swinging gold watch all day. 'Had a good day mesmerizing?' asks his devoted wife. Perhaps he gives her a slight smile, indicating that he did indeed persuade several people to sing 'Land of Hope and Glory' whilst standing on one leg; or perhaps he relates yet another tale of opposition and discouragement, like the attack from a vicar who told him, 'In my opinion you will never succeed lecturing on this subject. Your mouth is not the right shape.'

Despite the evidence that Powell was one of the unluckiest men who ever lived, the reader is continually reassured by his optimism. He believed that, unlike his writing, people could always get better. He was a keen supporter of education for the workers, giving many lectures and poetry readings at various institutes up and down the country. Here are his verses celebrating a 'soirée' held at the Wolverton Mechanics' Institute.

> We've met to celebrate, with social joy,
> Our Institution's Progress and its power,
> To wield a mightier influence o'er the mind,
> To speed the approaching jubilee of thought,

Set free from prejudice, and all
The powers that with deceptive dalliance blind
The soul's perception of the just *and* true.

Maybe it's just me, but this seems a tall order for the Wolverton Mechanics' Institute. The founders probably thought they were setting up a social club and now they find themselves speeding the jubilee of thought and setting the entire world free from prejudice.

Judging by the printed extracts, sitting through Powell's lectures cannot have been easy. This is the opening of his lecture on 'The Poetry of Feeling and Diction':

> *When the summer sun robes the creation in luxurious apparel, and the variegated flowers exhale delicious incense to the breeze – while, perchance, ever and anon the lark ascends the aërial passages of Heaven, intermingling its mellow voice with the surrounding atmosphere, and the whole feathered messengers of song make the country resound with strains of melodious music – when every tree bears its fruit and flower its bloom; what rapture fills the soul of man as he gazes around on such transcendent charms. What electric throbbings of joy vibrate the harp-strings of his heart.*

> *Who amongst us cannot echo these sentiments? Who of us has never heard the birdsong and felt the electric throbbing twang their heartstrings?*

Despite all this electrically-generated throbbing, Powell's finest moment lay not in his poems or his lectures, but in his only drama, 'The Compact'. This had but one performance – a solo reading which was disappointingly received and during which, with typically Powellian tragedy, one of the audience accidentally suffocated her own baby.

The drama tells of the relationship between Jessica, daughter of Sir Reginald Kingston, and Clarance Flemming, a blacksmith and poet. Jessica only knows Clarance as 'C.F.', the author of many fine and moving verses:

> JESSICA: I have been a-reading,
>   My dear father, more verses from the pen
>   Of C.F.; they are so rich in plaintive sweetness…

Sir Reginald, however, has no time for poets:

> SIR REGINALD: I'd have such knaves
>   Who idle time and blur paper with poems,
>   Confined as lunatics, 'till reason shone
>   Upon their pamby skulls.
>   Poets are mad,
>   And those are mad too, who dream their lives out
>   In poet studies.[2]

Eventually Jessica finds out who 'C.F.' actually is by interrogating his friend, the village idiot, Jerry Simple.

> JESSICA: Dost know, young man,
>   Thy friend's delights? I mean the themes that woo
>   His heart when freedom hushes toil?

> JERRY SIMPLE: I knows summat o' what he's fond o' loike. He
>   doesna' smoke, Miss, nor tak snuff, nor stagger whome drunk, if
>   that be what thee means.

> JESSICA: No, no, My faithful friend, I mean not so, pray tell me
>   Does he read?

> JERRY SIMPLE: Read, Miss, I should say as how he does and no
>   mistake, he's shopmates ca's he's a genyes or summet loike o' the
>   kin.

This is dialect of the highest order. Jessica and Clarance meet and embrace over a hot anvil. But their love is nearly thwarted by the villainous Captain Slix, a cad and a bounder who is so addicted to drink he even swears by the relevant Greek god.

> CAPTAIN SLIX: By Bacchus, she carries her pretty head high above
>   her shoulders.

[2] Any reader of this book will concede that Sir Reginald has a point.

In a shocking scene, Jessica is assaulted by Slix in the shrubbery:

> CAPTAIN SLIX: *Have no very peremptory objections to leaving you at the present moment, so don't mind going to oblige you, don't by Bacchus, but should rather like to present you with a pledge of affection, my unalterable affection, Jess, so just one kiss of those carnation lips –*

> JESSICA (frightened): *What mean you, Captain Slix? I trust my womanly weakness may save me from thy unhallowed touch.*

> CAPTAIN SLIX: *I'll 'ave just one kiss by Bacchus. (Seizes her hand, Jessica screams, Clarance, who is passing at the time, springs between them and prevents the Captain from carrying his threat into execution.)*

> CLARANCE: *For shame, man, have you no virtue in your nature? Or is it sold to gambling, debauchery and libertinism?*

Eventually Clarance is revealed to be the son of the Earl of Westlon, who is going through hard times. Happily, however, he goes to London, finds fame through his poetry and wins three hundred guineas in a novel-writing competition.

He returns to Wiltshire, meets a character with the wonderful name of Theophilus Sideglance and arrives at the hall just in time to stop Jessica taking poison and/or being forcibly married to Captain Slix.

One cannot help but feel there is an element of wish-fulfilment about the story of a blacksmith who writes poetry, wins a literary prize and is really the son of an earl. But we should not begrudge Powell his fantasy. His life was hard – indeed harder than he ever wrote about. At the end of his autobiography he declines to give an account of the past five or six years because it was so bizarre it would 'produce a book that might be taken for a novel'.

The mind boggles.

Bibliography

The Village Bridal and other Poems, London, 1854
Phases of Thought and Feeling, London, 1857
Timon & Other Poems, Brighton, 1859 (includes *The Compact*)
Powell's Domestic Magazine, Brighton, 1860
Life Incidents and Poetic Pictures, London, 1865

☞ Death, Disaster and Disease
Julia Moore; William MacGonagall; Eliza Cook; *Titanic* Poets; Amanda McKittrick Ros

☞ Plays and Verse Drama
William Nathan Stedman; Francis Saltus Saltus; Walter Reynolds

Eliza Cook (1818-89)
The Boadicea of Literature

As one of his never-ending schemes to make money, James Henry Powell founded *Powell's Domestic Magazine*, a monthly collection of stories, poems and homilies.[1] During the brief few months of its existence it came to the attention of another extremely bad writer, Eliza Cook. Ultimately it led to a meeting of titans, when Powell was summoned to meet the great woman. The meeting had its frosty moments, especially when Powell, confused by Cook's masculine appearance, got her gender mixed up:

> *During her conversation I so completely lost all idea of her sex that I suspended an answer to some question put by her, which I did not exactly hear, with a 'Sir?' which blunder caused a blush to mount to my face.*

After this mistake, he tried to make amends:

> *I spoke warmly of her poems and expressed an opinion that she had written nothing superior to 'The Old Armchair'. I ought to have qualified the remark. Her countenance betrayed dissatisfaction and she quickly replied, 'I should be very sorry, indeed, if I had written nothing superior to that.'*
>
> *I saw my mistake and hastily said, 'I mean for pathos, none of your more ambitious poems have taken such a hold as that has on the hearts of the people.'*
>
> *The remark pleased her. Her countenance changed and she said with animation, 'Do you know, when I wrote that poem the paper was flooded with tears.'*

---

[1] It went bust after five months.

The meeting sums up Eliza Cook so well – a mixture of pomposity and sentimentality, an unerring belief in her own artistry, whilst churning out poems on armchairs and hats and the evils of drink. The poem he refers to was Cook's most popular work:

I love it, I love it; and who shall dare
To chide me for loving that old Arm-chair?

She was fond of these rhetorical questions, as the beginning to 'The Englishmen' shows:

There's a land that bears a world-known name,
Though it is but a little spot;
I say 'tis first on the scroll of Fame
And who shall say it is not?

Not me. I wouldn't dare. It would be like arguing with Boadicea.

The titles of her poems give a good idea of their style – 'A Temperance Song', 'There's A Silver Lining To Every Cloud', 'Mother, Come Back', 'My Old Straw Hat'. All of them so sweet as to be positively sickly.

'Song of an Ugly Maiden' is obviously written from the heart:

Oh! why shouldst thou trace my shrinking face
With coarse, deriding jest?
Oh! why forget that a charmless brow
May abide with a gentle breast?
Oh! why forget that gold is found
Hidden beneath the roughest ground?

Yet lurking beneath this sentimentalism was a sense of the mysterious and the macabre. There was, perhaps, something gothic hidden under that rough ground:

The sweet and merry sunshine makes the very church-yard fair;
We half forget the yellow bones, while yellow flowers are there…

Her poem 'Song of the Sea Weed' might indicate a secret yearning to be Samuel Taylor Coleridge:

> *Many a lip is gaping for drink,*
> *And madly calling for rain;*
> *And some hot brains are beginning to think*
> *Of a messmate's opened vein.*

'There is Nothing in Vain', however, has more of Wordsworth about it:

> *There's a mission, no doubt, for the mole in the dust,*
> *As there is for the charger, with nostrils of pride;*
> *The sloth and the newt have their places of trust,*
> *And the agents are needed, for God has supplied.*

Not every poet has the vision to appreciate the newt's place in the cosmic scheme of things, nor the insight to appreciate the mission of the mole.

Like Powell, Eliza Cook did not limit herself to poetry. She too published a journal, from which a selection of pieces were culled and published as *Jottings From My Journal*. Throughout the pieces, like the Queen or Margaret Thatcher, she talks of herself in the plural.'We were sitting lately in our snuggery one evening…' she writes, and immediately the reader wants to fire-bomb the place, or insert her forcibly into her 'old arm-chair'. 'We are somewhat eccentric in our taste at times, and never ashamed of owning a vulgar admiration…'

In an article called 'Back Streets' she takes us into the seamy side of the city:

> *We have wended our steps into a somewhat desolate thoroughfare, and now let us look about us. The first point of notice is a beer shop … we see the swarthy artisan or ragged idler issuing thence, with the hectic flush of unhealthy excitement on his face, and the thick words of brainless folly on his lips; we shudder as we mark the helpless infant shrinking from its forced participation in the feverish draught of a reckless mother; we sigh to watch the poor man's child as he*

cautiously and feloniously appropriates a few mouthfuls from the bro-
ken jug he has been sent with to get filled at the Infernal fountain…

After the beer-shop (and a sentence lasting 255 words) we move on to the pawnbroker's, and it is here that Eliza's imagination really starts to run wild. Indeed, one suspects she might have been having a few sips from the Infernal fountain herself, or even a puff on the pipe of perdition. The sight of a pawned china tea-service conjures up a vision of domestic tragedy:

> *We can picture the family party, full of hope and health, draining the*
> *leaves in sober cheerfulness and telling fortunes in the 'grounds;' we*
> *can see the thick bread and butter prepared for the hungry 'boys and*
> *girls,' and we help ourselves to shrimps and watercresses while we*
> *admire the fairy birds and Eden flowers of Staffordshire production,*
> *peeping at us through the comestibles. And then we trace the coming*
> *paleness on the husband's face; he is weak, and cannot walk as many*
> *miles as he did; his employers cannot have a labourer unworthy of his*
> *hire, and he loses his respectable situation.*[2]

Within a matter of weeks their savings have gone and he is coughing all over his tea-service:

> *They have saved something but it is all going and he must have a doc-*
> *tor; the wife eats little that he may have more, but the last sixpence*
> *has been spent… We see the wife stealing out in the dusk with a large*
> *basket, – she hangs her head as she stops at a far-distant pawn-*
> *broker's; but it must be done, and a bold step or two carries the tea-*
> *service to the counter…*

After that it all goes downhill and she is in and out of the pawnbroker's like a rat down a drain.

Despite Eliza's heartfelt depiction, one gets the feeling that she is not writing from experience. The nearest, one imagines, she ever came to a back street was to drive past one in her large and no doubt comfortable carriage.

[2] This whole thing sounds like an episode from James Henry Powell's auto-biography.

In 'People Who Do Not Like Poetry', she launches a savage attack on anyone who dislikes verse. I am not sure about her opening line of argument – it is hard to see what is either 'useful' or 'necessary' about cholera, but she was obviously a bit upset:

> They may be useful and necessary – so may the cholera; but in honest simplicity, we desire to keep clear of both infections... 'People who do not like poetry' have rarely much participation in the elasticities of our lot. Eating, drinking, sleeping and 'looking to the main chance,' generally form their whole consecutive occupations ... if any occasional development of humour and cheerfulness occur in the genus, we have observed that it usually tends to 'practical joking and coarse badinage'... Some of them even advocate the strong practical joke of killing off the superfluous population...

One can't help but feel she is being a little harsh here. I have many friends who don't much like poetry, and I am pretty sure that none of them have ever butchered children. They might approve of butchering Eliza, but that is another matter.

Ultimately, for all her popularity – and she was popular – Eliza Cook faded as quickly as she bloomed. Her many books of poetry lie unopened in libraries and old bookshops.

Some of them may even have been pawned.

Bibliography

Jottings From My Journal, London, 1860
Collected Poems, London, 1864

☞ Death, Disaster and Disease
Julia Moore; William MacGonagall; James Henry Powell; *Titanic* Poets; Amanda McKittrick Ros

☞ Minor Victorians
Stephen Fawcett; Leopold John Manners De Michele; Alfred Austin; J. Stanyan Bigg; Pownoll Toker Williams

☞ Philosophy and Theology
Margaret Cavendish; The Devout Salutationist; 'Lord'
Timothy Dexter; William Nathan Stedman; Keith Odo
Newman

******

Reverend Edward Dalton (fl. 1866)

The Monet of the Steam Engine

W hereas Thomas Baker was the Leonardo da Vinci of steam – all engineering detail and design – Rev. Edward Dalton is more of an Impressionist. While Baker drew with fine precision the working of Rennie's conoidal triple-bladed screw, Dalton paints with broad brush strokes the noise and the bustle of the primitive railway.

The Sea, the Railway Journey and Other Poems is a thick volume containing a number of epic poems and some shorter religious lyrics, including the intriguingly named 'Broken Cisterns' which is presumably about plumbing.[1] He starts it by indicating that he hasn't really been trying hard:

> *It is not likely that many strangers will peruse this unpretending volume; and it is not necessary for me to inform my personal friends, who will constitute its principal readers, that I have not given my chief time or best mental vigour to the composition of poetry.*

I think he is being slightly disingenuous here. These poems are the work of a craftsman. 'The Railway Journey' is a poem of which Proust would be proud; we are told the poet's waking habits, what he had for breakfast, what he was wearing – in fact it takes seven pages before he even gets to the station:

> *And when our feet have passed the portal,*
> *Are we on earth? and are our senses mortal?*
> *What sounds of fear*
> *Assail our ear,*

---

[1] Actually it isn't. I think it's something to do with the prophet Isaiah.

> What sights surprise
> Our dazzled eyes!
> From every quarter
> Cries of 'Porter,'
> Ladies falling
> Babies squalling
> Children racing
> Tearing, chasing,
> Servants rushing,
> Bonnets crushing...

The station is like something out of Dante. Flash swells loaf about, rustic workmen stand there with straws in their mouths, old men hobble by; there are even, in a rather xenophobic passage, some 'tawdry smart Frenchmen', 'Dull German clowns',

> Bloated Dutch skippers, redolent of Gin
> and lanky scarecrows with a yanky grin.

Eventually we get on to the train:

> At length like seamen from the boiling surge
> Half choked and stifled I with pain emerge,
> From this most stormy sea
> With dislocated knees,
> With ankle sprained
> And raiment stained
> With hat most sadly shattered
> And ribs most sorely battered,
> With shins contused
> And elbows bruised,
> With spirits saddened,
> Feelings maddened
> To find myself in spite of patent guard
> Minus a watch and plus an inch of card.

I must admit that by the time we get this far, the reader is thinking that Rev. Dalton got everything he deserved; indeed we are half hoping that, like Huskisson, he will get his toga tangled up and fall under the wheels of the 6.06 to Paddington. Once he gets on the train, things get even noisier and the Reverend is reduced to a state of illiteracy:

> The last friends part
> And off we start
> The engine pants and snorts and blows
> The carriage doorways slam and close
> The broad and ponderous wheels are rolled
> By thick-set arms of iron mould,
> While streaming from the spouting side
> The steam escapes in hissing tide.
> Cranch, crunch, thud, rud, dubber-dub-rub,
> Thudder, rubber, dub-dub, dub-a-rub-rub-rub.

This, it has to be said, is fine writing. Never has a poet rubbed more dubbers. Still, he is obviously shocked by the experience. Presumably he has lived his life in his country rectory, emerging once a week to deliver a sermon on 'Plumbing in the Prophets'. Now he finds himself on a hissing monster, where everything makes a noise:

> Startled at starting for our nerves are weak,
> We gasp for breath,
> grow pale as death,
> As one long piercing, shrill, unearthly shriek
> Rings thro' our ears, and stops the power to speak,
> The cry of anguish or vindictive yell
> Of baffled imp, or vanquished fiend of hell,
> The death shriek of some monstrous beast,
> We've smashed a million pigs at least.
> Ah no! no sucking pig has lost a bristle,
> The shriek was but the starting railway whistle.
> ...
> Crash! crash! what's that? a peal of thunder?
> A rattling volley? No, a bridge we've just passed under.

Eventually they reach their destination, and, with relief, the Reverend can be shot of all these awful people:

> *We reach the station near the chosen spot,*
> *Where fields are common and policemen not:*
> *Through the long train from front to distant rear,*
> *Three thousand throats with loud and ringing cheer,*
> *Shout their arrival at the destined goal,*
> *and through the gates in surging torrents roll,*
> *As oozing mud from some discharging drain...*

Rev. Dalton did not limit his poetry merely to land travel. 'The Sea' is a massive poem that covers every aspect of maritime interest. Unlike 'The Railway Journey', however, it contains no rub-a-dubs to cheer it up. However, there is a stanza which strikes an almost decadent note. He praises the sea for

> *Producing from thy womb a boundless store*
> *Of food for man of every clime and shore,*
> *A thousand dishes of substantial fare,*
> *Nutritious esculents and dainties rare.*

I don't know what an esculent is, but as it came from the sea's womb I think I'll just throw it back.

Bibliography

The Sea, The Railway Journey and Other Poems, London, 1866

☞ Falero-lero-loo, Riddlety-diddlety Poets
George Wither; Rev. William Cook; James Whitcomb Riley; Théophile Marzials

☞ Boats and Trains
Thomas Baker; Frederick James Johnston-Smith; *Titanic* Poets

'Child' Poems

The 'Child' Poem was a particularly noxious carbuncle on the bottom of nineteenth-century poetry. In an attempt to be sweet, poets would write in the most twee manner possible. In most cases, the effect was merely to make the child sound as though he or she had a speech defect; a notable triumph it is true, but hardly the effect the poet was looking for. Here are three excellent examples:

James Whitcomb Riley

> An' Bang! bang! bang! we heerd the door –
> Nen it flewed open, an' the floor
> Blowed full o' snow – that's first we saw,
> Till little Lee-Bob shriek' at Ma
> 'There's Santy Claus! – I know him by
> His big white mufftash!' – an ist cry
> An' laugh an' squeal an' dance an' yell…
> from 'A Defective Santa Claus'

Bertha Moore (fl. 1890s)

> If I were God, up in the sky,
> I'll tell you all vat I would do,
> I would not let the babies cry
> Because veir tooths was coming froo.
> I'd make them born wif tooths all white,
> And curly hair upon veir heads
> And so vat vey could sit upright
> Not always lie down in veir beds.
> from 'A Child's Thought'

Fred Emerson Brooks

Tind friends, I pray extuse me
   From matin' any speech,
Betause I is so 'ittle
   I ain't dot much for each;
There ain't much edutation
   In such a 'ittle head;
Besides, I is so s'eepy
   An' wants to do to bed.

from 'The New Baby'

***

Edward Edwin Foot (fl. 1867)
Master of the Footnote

Given his name, perhaps it was fate that led Edward Edwin Foot to his particular area of specialization. For this unassuming officer in Her Majesty's Customs was the supreme master of the footnote.

Edward Edwin raised (or possibly lowered, depending on your point of view) the footnote to an art form. No poem was left without annotation, no metaphor unexplained. His footnotes were often verbose, frequently pointless and sometimes even longer than the poem.

He wrote only one book, *Original Poems of Edward Edwin Foot of Her Majesty's Customs*. The footnotes begin on the very first line:

The Author* of the present volume…

_____

*A native of Ashburton, Devonshire.

He was, apparently, pathologically unable to leave his poems alone. Even the titles were explained:

Raven Rock[1]
Some summer's day, upon that rock –
A cliff, wherein the ravens flock
List ye to the Dart,[2] below;
See the little rapids flow: –
From that proud stream no discords rise;
No shipwrecks e'er bedim our eyes.
Oft have I[3] watch'd, thereon, its course,
(Astride the rock as 'twere a horse)

Singing o'er a favourite song,
Twice and thrice to make it long…

---

[1]*Raven Rock is about 500 feet above and near the banks of the River Dart; it is distant about two and a half miles from Ashburton, Devonshire, and bounded on the north side by Aswell Woods from which it is easily accessible.*

[2]*The Dart river whose source is in the forest of Dartmoor, is most appropriately called the 'English Rhine'. The scenery in the locality of 'Raven Rock' is very beautiful.*

[3]*The author of the poem.*

It is the utter pointlessness of his footnotes that is so appealing – no one else would bother to point out that the word 'I' in the poem above signified the author, but to Edward Edwin, nothing should be left to chance.

In many ways he was the least poetic poet ever. Not because he could not think of poetic images, but because having thought of them, he couldn't bear to leave them unexplained. Later in the poem we read:

The Captain scans the ruffled zone[1]

to which Foot adds the helpful footnote:

[1] *A figurative expression, intended by the author to signify the horizon.*

The same poem shows his mastery of one of the key skills of the bad poet, the pointless apostrophe:

At last the Captain in despair,
Exhorts the passengers t'attend
Unto his last few words of prayer, –
To meet their 'nevitable end!

For hours the pumps in vain were mann'd,
As tenfold did the waters rise;

> *The pumpers frenzically scann'd * * **
> *And some, unnerv'd, betear'd their eyes.*

Strangely, given his penchant for explaining everything in sight, the author does not explain the significance of the three asterisks at the end of the line.

He was a patriotic figure, given to celebrating royal events. The opening of this poem on the arrival of Her Royal Highness Princess Alexandra gives the impression she had indigestion:

> *She left her parents weepingly, –*
> *The parting gave her bosom pain...*

However, he is soon into his stride, with a wonderfully bad piece of verse that, as well as benefiting from some pointless footnotes, also produces some powerful imagery. No reader can easily forget this picture of the young, painfully bosomed princess, cascading love-crystals everywhere and apparently falling over as soon as she reaches the deck:

> *But hope re-cheer'd her o'er the main,*
> *For Edward 'waited anxiously*
> *Fair Princess Alexandra.*
> *Christening the Prince[1]*
> *One circle round our Sun – and o'er –*
> *Is perfected, since forth there stray'd[2]*
> *In youth a fair Princess,*
> *From whom fell liquid drops of love –*
> *Love-crystals of her wedding tour.*
> *Though griev'd, the fair-form'd gentle maid*
> *(Whom God was pleased to bless),*
> *With modest courage sweetly strove*
> *And conquer'd it! – Joy helping her.*
> *Those moments sad, Time soon spent out:*
> *Her Edward, yet afar,*
> *Beheld her with bright vision's eye.*
> *She wiped away the pearly tear,*
> *And tripp'd on deck.*

---

[1] *The reader will please to observe that lines 1st and 5th, 2nd and 6th, 3rd and 7th, etc., have rhythmical terminations.*

[2] *The author seeks indulgence in using the word 'stray'd'.*

It is helpful of Foot to point out the rhyme scheme, but I still don't know why he asks our pardon for the word 'stray'd'.

Few facts are known about him. He was born on 5 January 1828 at Ashburton in Devon, the fifth son of Peter Foot. He married a Miss Hext and on 11 June 1858 began his career with the customs service in London. At some time in his life he appears to have made a voyage to Australia, judging from the amount of detail in the footnotes to his poem 'The Homeward Bound Passenger Ship'.

> *Down yonder hatchway, in the shade*
> *The dice or cards are nimbly dealt;*
> *While those who move them oft degrade*
> *Themselves by adding sin to guilt.*
> *Whilst further aft, in best of hope,*
> *A group[1] seem pompous o'er their gain;*
> *The saffron liquid freely tope,*
> *And whisk the bottles in the main.*

---

[1] *Perchance a party of lucky adventurers; such, for instance, as three or four fortunate diggers, who probably had worked as a company on some gold field in Australia, and were returning to their native country.*

Sometimes he uses his footnotes to explain to his readers the complexities of his craft. His poem 'On Shakespeare' has the following footnote:

NOTE. – The reader is requested to observe that lines 1–5, 2–6, 3–7, 4–8 (and so on in every eight consecutive lines), have rhythmical terminations, though the quantity of feet do not agree, but the number of feet in lines 1–9, 2–10, 3–11, 4–12, 5–13, 6–14, 7–15, and 8–16 (and so in each successive 16 lines) will be found to correspond, with but slight variation.

It is only when you figure out the rhyme scheme that you realize he has rhymed 'forgott'n' with 'trodd'n', 'him' with 'beam', and best of all, 'utter' with 'stature'. With a talent of this magnitude, it was a tragedy that he only produced one book. After *Original Poems*, he devoted his life to Her Majesty's Customs, where his attention to detail and his precise definitions were put to more commercial, if less poetic use.

Edward Edwin Foot was perfectly named to indulge in the creative use of footnotes. And it raises some intriguing possibilities, for maybe there are others, similarly selected by fate. It would be nice to think that somewhere, a Henry Sonnet is scribbling away, that Mrs Edith Shortstory is perfecting her skills and that, one day, the world will welcome a truly awful reference work by the hitherto unknown Boris Bibliography?

Bibliography

Original Poems of Edward Edwin Foot of Her Majesty's Customs, London, London, 1867

☞ Poets of Royalty
Joseph Gwyer; Alfred Austin

Alfred Austin (1835–1913)
Britain's Worst Poet Laureate

In the British television series *Yes Minister*, there is a wonderful moment when the hero, the hapless Jim Hacker, becomes Prime Minister. He attains this high honour not because of his leadership qualities, but because he *lacks* all leadership qualities. The civil service want a man entirely without drive and initiative; they want someone they can control. Jim Hacker, inoffensive, inept, is a perfect candidate.

This fictional episode bears an uncanny likeness to the real story of Alfred Austin, the man who became Poet Laureate by default. When Tennyson died, the government cast around for replacements. Queen Victoria, discussing the matter with Gladstone,[1] is reputed to have said, 'I am told that Mr Swinburne is the best poet in my dominions,' which raises the intriguing prospect of a sado-masochistic Poet Laureate with a penchant for lesbianism and flagellation.[2]

In the event it was left to another PM, Lord Salisbury, to make the decision. Of the front runners, none was an obvious choice. Swinburne was a pervert; Morris was, even worse, a Socialist; Patmore was a Catholic and Kipling was presumably too busy with his cake factory. Thus it was that Salisbury turned to one of his own kind. He offered the job to a political crony – Alfred Austin, a leader writer for the Conservative paper *The Standard* and the author of some

---

[1] Or the Antichrist, as he is better known (see pp. 223ff.).

[2] Of course, I can't guarantee that there *hasn't* been a sado-masochistic Poet Laureate with a penchant for lesbianism and flagellation, but I can't see any obvious candidates. I cannot, for example, imagine John Betjeman in leather and brandishing a whip. Well, I can, but I'd rather not…

wonderfully bad verse.

'He has floated in at last to the Laureateship on the strength of a prose volume about his garden in Kent', wrote Wilfred Scawen Blunt, and it is certainly difficult to see how his poetry could have earned him the post. His first book, *Randolph, A Tale of Polish Grief*, supposedly sold a mere seventeen copies. It was followed with a series of largely forgotten books of verse, Austin supporting himself mainly on his journalistic work.

Nevertheless, he *was* a poet and his verse *was* published and that, in Lord Salisbury's eyes, was enough. And of Austin's conservatism there was no doubt – he was, for a start, virulently francophobic, writing about them

> *O thou nation, base-besotted, whose ambition cannon shotted,*
> *And huge mounds of corpses clotted with cold gore alone can sate!*
> *May the God of Battles shiver every arrow in thy quiver,*
> *And the nobly flowing river thou dost covet drown thy hate.*
> from 'The Challenge Answered'

Whilst being anti-French is virtually a national pastime of the English, it does seem a bit much to accuse them of consuming gore, clotted or otherwise.

His conservatism also extended to clothing. Take, for example, his principled and passionate attack on the padded bra:

> *And do they wear that lubricating lie,*
> *That fleshless falsehood! Palpitating maids*
> *Puff themselves out with hollow buxomness,*
> *To lead some breathless gaby [sic] at their heels*
> *A scentless paper chase!*

These lines – spoken by a country girl called Urania – come from his verse drama *Fortunatus the Pessimist*. Urania is depicted at work in the country, where her father Franklin runs a farm:

> *He tends the kine; Urania brims the pail*

> *Coaxing the udders with her lissom fingers*
> *Sweet as the milk they drain…*
> *… A wimple on her head, and kirtled short*
> *She pegs the snow-white linen in the wind,*
> *And, singing back her way into the threshold*
> *Compounds the custard…*

No wonder she didn't need padding – she probably slipped a bit of compounded custard down there instead.

Another major work of his was 'The Human Tragedy', a poem he revised no less than four times, but still managed to leave relatively appalling:

> *A duller dinner never was devoured*
> *The dishes passed, the conversation flagged;*
> *Mary by silent stupor was o'er powered,*
> *Dumb were her parents, even Hubert gagged.*

It seems to me like an early case of carbon monoxide poisoning. Or possibly he was choking on a bit of compounded custard.

One of his more appealing early works is 'Rome or Death!', a romantic verse which features a strangely juicy heroine called Miriam:

> *Her body was of glorious make; her limbs*
> *Vaunted the strain of that Olympian line,*
> *Reared upon earth as sung in deathless hymns*
> *When mortal mould was filled with juice divine.*

Sloshing slightly, she approaches the hero, Godrid, and tempts him with her grapes:

> *…as she came anear, the juicy bells*
> *She merrily held and dangled in his face.*

Naturally, he has no defence against either her juicy bells or her juicy body and together they rush off to invade Italy:

> *Then out they sprang – first Miriam, Gilbert next,*
> *Last Godfrid, – and the eager host pressed round;*

> Rude fishermen, hoarse women half unsexed
> And rude sea-urchins, frisking o'er the ground...

It is not made clear how the sea-urchins managed to be rude and frisky – I should have thought that either occupation was beyond your average sea-urchin. And the picture of the fishermen and the women is rather unpleasant, although I dare say that if a sea-urchin was frisking near you, you might be rude about it. After all, those things are sharp.

Although most of his writing is mind-numbingly dull, at his best Austin is gloriously dreadful. That a man should be Poet Laureate who can make rhymes like the following is one of the lasting joys of English literature:

> Through these, through all I first did see,
>   With me to share my raptures none,
> That nuptialled Monica would be
>   My novice and companion.

And he could never be less than the conservative, prim and proper Victorian. His poem 'A Sleepless Night' implies that the entire universe runs like a railway timetable:

> Within the hollow silence of the night
> I lay awake and listened. I could hear
> Planet with punctual planet chiming clear...[3]

Happily, unlike so many better poets, his appointment as Laureate did not adversely affect the quality of his work. It remained as bad as ever. His first work after the appointment was a poem on the Jamestown Raid which annoyed Queen Victoria:[4]

> So we forded and galloped forward,
> As hard as our beasts could pelt,

[3] Say what you like about God, but at least the planets run on time.
[4] The poem annoyed her, not the raid. Well, I suppose the raid may have annoyed her as well, but probably not as much as the poem.

First eastward, then trending northward,
Right over the rolling veldt.

Some have claimed that becoming Laureate was the worst moment in Austin's life, opening him up to a torrent of abuse and mockery that was to continue to his death. However, he does not seem to have viewed it that way. With the sublime self-confidence of the truly bad, he really believed that it had been earned by merit, that he actually was at the head of English literature.

To lovers of poetry his appointment was a slap in the face, a complete devaluation of the post of Poet Laureate. To those who enjoy bad verse, however, it remains a decision of which the government could be proud and a complete vindication of Austin, his poetry, his juicy heroines and his wonderful compounding custard.

Bibliography

Too much to mention, frankly. Try *Fortunatus the Pessimist* (London, 1892) and see how far you get.

☞ Minor Victorians
Eliza Cook; Stephen Fawcett; Leopold John Manners De Michele; J. Stanyan Bigg; Pownoll Toker Williams

☞ Poets of Royalty
Joseph Gwyer; Edward Edwin Foot

James Whitcomb Riley (1849–1916)
The Hoosier Poet

Astonishingly, James Whitcomb Riley was one of the most popular poets of his day. The preface to his *Poems* (1913) suggests that 'his poems deserve to be better known...' which is a sentiment that many would disagree with, especially in the light of 'A Nonsense Rhyme':

> Ringlty-Jing!
> And what will we sing?
> Some little crinkety-crankety thing
> That rhymes and chimes,
> And skips sometimes,
> As though wound up with a kink in the spring.
>
> Grunkety-krung!
> And chunkety-plung!
> Sing the soul that the bullfrog sung, –
> A song of the soul
> Of a mad tadpole
> That met his fate in a leaky bowl:
> And it's O for the first false wiggle he made
> In the sea of pale pink lemonade!

Riley's forte was the dialect poem, a form which even Kipling found difficult, never mind the author of 'Little Orphant Annie'.

> Little Orphant Annie's come to our house to stay,
> An' wash the cups an' saucers up an' bresh the crumbs away,
> An' shoo the chickens off the porch, an' dust the hearth an' sweep,
> An' make the fire an' bake the bread an' earn her board an' keep;
> An' all us other children, when the supper things is done,

> We set around the kitchen fire an' has the mostest fun
> A-listenin' to the witch tales 'at Annie tells about.
> An' the gobble-uns 'at gits you
>   Ef you
>   Don't
>   Watch
>   Out!

The moral comes with thudding steps:

> You'd better mind yer parunts, and yer teachers fond and dear,
> An' churish them 'at loves you, an' dry the orphant's tear
> An' he'p the pore an' needy ones 'at clusters all about,
> Er the gobble-uns'll git you
>   Ef you
>   Don't
>   Watch
>   Out!

Born in Greenfield, Indiana, James's father Reuben – wisely some might say – did not encourage his poetry.

> My father did not encourage my verse-making for he thought it too visionary, and being a visionary himself, he believed he understood the dangers of following the promptings of the poetic temperament. I doubted if anything would come of the verse-writing myself.

Not so much 'visionary', more 'hallucinatory' in my opinion. Here is the first verse of one of his many children's poems:

> The Crankadox leaned o'er the edge of the moon
>   And wistfully gazed on the sea
> Where the Gryxabodill madly whistled a tune
>   To the air of 'Ti-fol-de-ding-dee'.
> The quavering shriek of the Fly-up-the-creek
>   Was fitfully wafted afar
> To the Queen of the Wunks as she powdered her cheek
>   With the pulverized rays of a star.
> from Craqueodoom

Personally I think his father didn't try hard enough. Maybe locking him in a cellar might have saved us all such torment.

Riley started work in his father's law office, but soon switched to journalism and his first poetry appeared in 1872 in the *Indianapolis Saturday Mirror*.

He was later fired from one job for forging a 'lost' poem by Edgar Allen Poe, but with the publication of his dialect poems he found popular success. From there it was all down-hill – or down the pan – depending on how you look at it.

His dialect poems earned him the name of 'The Hoosier Poet', from the region where he was born and whose accents he borrowed. As time went on, however, he looked further afield for his 'voices'. 'Dot Leedle Boy' for example, is a poem told in a sort of Dutch dialect. At least I think it's Dutch. It could be German. Or even Swahili.

> *Ot's a leedle Gristmas story*
> > *Dot I told der leedle folks –*
> *Und I vant you stop dot laughin'*
> > *Und grackin' funny jokes! –*
> *So help me Peter-Moses!*
> > *Ot's no time for monkey-shine,*
> *Ober I vast told you somedings*
> > *Of dot leedle boy of mine!*

And 'tell us somedings' he does. For verse after verse after verse. Thankfully, after a while the 'leedle boy' catches pneumonia and dies. Not before seeing Father Christmas apparently:

> *I told you, friends – dot's someding,*
> > *Der last time dot he speak*
> *Und say, 'GOOT-BY, KRISS KRINGLE!'*
> > *– Dot make me feel so veak*
> *I yoost kneel down und drimble*[1]*,*
> > *Und bur-sed out a-gryin',*
> *'MEIN GOTT, MEIN GOTT IN HIMMEL! –*
> > *DOT LEEDLE BOY OF MINE!'*

[1] He means either 'tremble' or 'dribble'. Or perhaps she was doing both.

One can just imagine him reciting this at one of his many performances. I bet there wasn't a dry eye in the house. Or a dry seat, come to that.

His poems celebrated not only the people, but the landscape of Indiana. 'A Summer Afternoon' features some rather asthmatic wind:

> A languid atmosphere, a lazy breeze,
> With labored respiration, moves the wheat

While in 'Honey Dripping from the Comb' the reader is left to wonder what on earth is making all the oohing noises in the woods:

> How slight a thing may set one's fancy drifting
> Upon the dead sea of the Past! – A view –
> Sometimes an odor – or a rooster lifting
> A far-off 'OOH! OOH-OOH!'

Call me 'Mr. Suspicious' but I don't think that's a rooster. I reckon that's the Crankadox and the Queen of the Wunks having a bit of a chunkety-plung.

Whatever we think of his poetry nowadays, he became incredibly famous and hugely loved. So much so that when he died over 35,000 people filed past his coffin in the Indiana State Capitol.[2] His home is now a museum and he has a children's hospital named after him. There is even a festival in his honour. Grown men are still reduced to tears by poems such as 'When the Frost is on the Punkin' and 'The Happy Little Cripple'.

For me, his most moving poem is 'The Smitten Purist'. But I would rather not state which part of me is actually moved.

---

[2] Although they may just have been making sure he was dead.

Thweet Poethy! let me lithp forthwith
That I may thhing of the name of Smith –
    which name, alath!
    In harmony hath
No adequate rhyme, letht you grant me thith –
That the thimple, thibillant thound of eth –
(Which to thave my thoul, I cannot expreth!)
Thuth I may thhingingly,
Wooingly and winningly
Thu-thu-thound in the name of Smith.

Stuttering and lisping. Truly, this man's genius knew no bounds.

Bibliography

Complete Poetry in Ten Volumes, New York, 1913

☞ Dialects and Accents
J. Stanyan Bigg; 'Child' Poems; Amanda McKittrick Ros

☞ Falero-lero-loo, riddlety-diddlety poets
George Wither; Rev. William Cook; Théophile Marzials

The Five Golden Rules of Bad Writing
3. All Criticism Is Based on Envy

What has always astonished me about truly great bad writers is that they remained undaunted in the face of criticism, ridicule and, frequently, physical assault. They are immune to adverse criticism – indeed, they often seem to thrive on it. I think it is because, in their minds, criticism is directly linked to genius. 'All great artists are ridiculed,' they reason, 'therefore the more I am ridiculed, the greater an artist I must be.'

And so, far from discouraging them, opposition, criticism and even abuse only confirms their standing in the world of literature.

For example . . .
Amanda McKittrick Ros, writing about *Irene Iddlesleigh*, was convinced of its greatness:

> *I am pleased to say that this work now rests upon the shelf of 'Classic', for which reason I presume the critics, lately, have done their utmost to murder both the Book and its Author: nevertheless I – still – live & this book shall never die.*

While Julia Moore attacked her detractors in terms that have passion, if not grammar:

> *Thanks to the Editors that has spoken in favour of my writings; may they ever be successful. The Editors that has spoken in a scandalous manner have went beyond reason . . .*

The Golden Age

****

Théophile Marzials (1850–1924)
Author of the Worst Poem Ever

I remember, as if it were yesterday, the excitement I felt in turning over the pages of the manuscript notebook.[1] Here was a new poem by one of the all-time greats. Here, in a dusty manuscript, written in his own hand, was an undiscovered poem by Théophile Marzials.

Marzials is the man who, some claim, wrote the worst poem ever. This was called, appropriately enough, 'A Tragedy' and is a wonderfully moving work. It begins with a dramatic opening:

> *DEATH!*
> *Plop.*
> *The barges down in the river flop.*
> *Flop, plop.*
> *Above, beneath.*
> *From the slimy branches the grey drips drop,*
> *As they scraggle black on the thin grey sky,*
> *Where the black cloud rack-hackles drizzle and fly*
> *To the oozy waters, that lounge and flop*
> *On the black scrag piles, where the loose cords plop,*
> *As the raw wind whines in the thin tree-top.*
> *Plop, plop.*
> *And scudding by*
> *The boatmen call out hoy! and hey!*
> *All is running water and sky,*
> *And my head shrieks – 'Stop,'*
> *And my heart shrieks – 'Die.'*

---

[1] Mainly because it *was* yesterday.

After this entertaining and somewhat nautical start, the poet
starts to drain himself:

My thought is running out of my head;
My love is running out of my heart,
My soul runs after, and leaves me as dead,
For my life runs after to catch them – and fled
They all are every one! – and I stand, and start,
At the water that oozes up, plop and plop,
On the barges that flop
   And dizzy me dead.
I might reel and drop.
     Plop.
     Dead.

And the shrill wind whines in the thin tree-top
   Flop, plop.

If you have never heard a wind make the noise 'flop, plop',
then you obviously haven't been listening hard enough. By
now the reader is a little unsure exactly what is causing all
this plopping about, but the solution comes in the final section. He has been betrayed by a 'friend' and within moments
the 'plops' have been replaced with 'ughs'.

A curse on him.
      Ugh! yet I knew – I knew –
If a woman is false can a friend be true?
It was only a lie from beginning to end –
    My Devil – My 'Friend'
I had trusted the whole of my living to!
  Ugh! and I knew!
   Ugh!
So what do I care,
And my head is empty as air –
   I can do,
   I can dare,
  (Plop, plop

> The barges flop
> Drip drop.)
>   I can dare! I can dare!
> And let myself all run away with my head[2]
> And stop.
>   Drop.
>   Dead.
>   Plop, flop.
>
>   Plop.

There. I warned you it was a moving experience. The poem is characteristic of Marzials's style, with its repetitive phrasing, gloriously strange noises and incomprehensible subject matter. And it is, of course, immensely moving, especially the resonance of that final 'plop, flop', then silence, then 'plop'. 'What has happened?' the reader is forced to ask. 'Has he run away with his own head? Has he jumped from the bridge, only to find the tide was out?' 'A Tragedy' is probably the greatest plopping poem in the history of literature, but it is just one of many superbly bad poems in Marzials's book, excitingly entitled *The Gallery Of Pigeons, And Other Poems*.

Marzials was born at Bagnères de Bigorre in France. His father was a Methodist minister who brought his family to England when he became the pastor of the French Protestant church in London. Although christened Théophile, he anglicized his name to Theophilus Julian Henry Marzials, or Theo for short. He was a very handsome man with 'yellow hair and yellow moustaches tinged with red, fine blue eyes, a cheerful wit, and an exceptionally attractive singing voice'.

In 1870 Theo joined the staff of the British Museum as a junior assistant in the principal librarian's office. His years at the library were mostly uneventful, although there was one notorious incident when, believing that the chief librarian was absent, he leant out from one of the galleries and cried

---

[2] Critical debate rages over this line. As to what it means, frankly, your guess is as good as mine.

'Am I or am I not the Department's darling?' Alas, the fearsome chief had returned early. He gave one look at Marzials, who simply fled, and 'the sound of his footsteps was heard echoing up the metal stairways till they seemed to fade away into infinity'.

Although the museum authorities discouraged 'versewriting and publishing' there were many poets working there at the time, including Coventry Patmore, Richard Garnett, Arthur O'Shaughnessy and Edmund Gosse. And it wasn't long before Theo joined them with a poem called *Passionate Dowsabella*, privately printed in 1872.

Passionate Dowsabella (A Pastoral) is a wonderful poem, a rural epic of love, lust, silly names and fennel.The poem begins with Dowsabella wandering through a lush landscape:

> *Dowsabella, Dowsabella, whither are you going?*
> *All alone along the meads where all the kine are lowing,*
> *Round the porch the white rose buds, their rich cream-heads*
>   *out-blowing*
> *Scents delicious, nod and beck, their fairest sister knowing,*
> *Winding down the long grey grass, where sing the men a-mowing,*
> *Winds the downy river on, with water weeds a-flowing...*

And so on, through all the matching rhymes such as 'upgrowing', 'a-going', 'showing' and then 'going' again. It is not long before Dowsabella finds herself up to her arms in fennel, which she apparently finds extremely stimulating:

> *Dowsabel, sweet Dowsabel,*
> *(She who loved and loved so well),*
> *Where the white-green fennel-bed*
> *Cast about its films and feathers,*
> *Sighing, laughing, wanderëd....*
>
> *Round her cream-white arms a-clinging;*
> *Round her, and round her, tight'ning and stringing;*
>   *Green-white, pearl-white, cream-white, rose-white*
>   *Glimmering,*

> *Shimmering;*
> *White to her flesh the white light springing,*
> *Up the fennel a-flying and flinging,*
>   *Tangled and tossing in light sharp tethers;*
> *While from far so clear came ringing*
>   *All the bells of those merry wethers!*

Dowsabella then enters an orchard and the man who previously rhymed 'fennel-bed' with 'wanderëd' scores another direct hit:

> *What's that look of maddening hunger,*
> *As if sharp some quick sting stung her?*

Dowsabella, it transpires, is in love, and, this being the late nineteenth century, it is not long before bosoms make an appearance.[3] In the following extract, Marzials does not tell us if both bosoms were hot and cold at the same time or if, conveniently, she had one hot and one cold like some Pre-Raphaelite drinks machine.

> *Thus did Dowsabella sigh;*
>   *And her arms along her breast*
>   *Writhed and tighten'd in, and press'd,*
> *Till the wrenching of her hand*
> *Crackled off the light green band, –*
>   *Leapt a tapering bosom out,*
>   *As a blossom curls about*
>   *Till the green bud bursts, and out*
>   *Runs the red-white poppy sprout.*
> *Dowsabel! Oh, Dowsabel!*
> *Methinks she loved him wond'rous well,*
> *For down her bosom hot and cold*
> *With love and fever, and fair to behold,*
> *Fell forth his flower of the marigold –*
> *In stripes of yellow and brown and gold.*

[3] Marzials, like other poets of the time such as Saltus and Austin, was obsessed with bosoms. Which is curious, because he was not that way inclined at all, preferring the company of young men.

Before long her lover arrives, causing her bosoms to drum like an over-excited rhythm section:

> *Who can doubt he kept the tryst?*
> *Who can doubt her mouth was kiss'd,*
> *Till its beauty rippled o'er?*
> *That her bosom-beats grew stronger*
> *Till their strength could hold no longer…*

And the section ends with fennel flying everywhere.

In part II it is autumn. We are introduced to Blowselind, a girl who is described as 'Large, and calm, and white and red' – an image which makes one think reluctantly of a dairy cow. Blowselind is loved by Lubin – the bloke, it transpires, who so shamelessly covered Dowsabella with his marigold back in the summer. He has now transferred his affection, if not his marigold, to Blowselind, a woman described, unsurprisingly, as 'broad-bosom'd'.[4]

At the harvest festival, Blowselind and Lubin dance watched by the spurned Dowsabella:

> *As foot to foot, and hand to hip*
> *Her love and hate went turn and trip,*
> *Now before and now behind,*
> *Now Lubin, now large Blowselind…*

Not unnaturally, Dowsabella, whose breasts are now 'huddled higher', is driven to madness. She has lost her love to a larger lady. The show is over and the fat lady has danced. Dowsabella leaves Lubin to his enormous paramour and runs through the snow into the graveyard, down to the icy river:

> *Dowsabella, through the silence, crackled through the crickling*
> *sedge;*
> *Shrinking – ever shrinking – huddled downward to the water's edge,*
> *Down the low slope where the rushes, torn and wither'd, freeze and*
> *shake,*
> *Glittering as her body's writhings through the tanglenesses break…*

[4] As opposed, presumably, to Dowsabella's 'tapering' numbers.

Eventually she walks into the river and drowns herself. Still at least, it being winter, she didn't have to wade through any more fennel.

Marzials followed this triumph with the aforementioned *The Gallery of Pigeons*, printed in 1873. The book takes its title from the first poem in the collection – a rather obscure work, which seems to liken the working of the imagination to the act of keeping a pigeon loft. Still, it does contain a memorable chorus:

> *Hyüeèps, Hyüeèps, Hyüeèps, Oho!*
> *Out, my pretties! Ho! my pretties!*
> *Cooing, cooing love and ditties!*
> *Losing you were worst of pities*
> *Ho! my pets and pretties, Ho!*

I have tried saying 'Hyüeèps, Hyüeèps, Hyüeèps' for many days now but, apart from getting my tongue stuck to the roof of my mouth, I can't understand how this noise should sound, nor why it should be attractive to pigeons.

The Gallery, it has to be admitted, contains a number of rather dull, imitative verses, but every now and then, as in 'A Tragedy' and *Dowsabella*, the true Marzials leaps out. 'The Sun of my Songs' contains one of his finest stanzas:

> *Yet all your song*
> *Is – 'Ding, dong,*
> * Summer is dead,*
> * Spring is dead –*
> *O my heart, and O my head!*
> *Go a-singing a silly song,*
> * All wrong,*
> *   For all is dead,*
> *   Ding, dong*
> *   And I am dead,*
> *   Dong!'*

It is that final 'dong' that is the mark of the true master. Many lesser poets would have lacked his courage, but Marzials was never afraid to dong, or even plop, where necessary. Another poem, 'Gabrielle', appears to be about a woman who stuffs a dove down her vest:

> *But she the while, as one with little care,*
> *With courbent fingers strove*
> > *To snap the pin*
> > *Of rubies and let bare*
> *The lawn about her boddice [sic], and therein*
> *To fondel-fold her dove.*

In one section of the book there is the odd story of a real, live angel who visits a carved stone angel on a church tower:

> *And thirsting at so tasty sight*
> *Came nigh and touch'd her bosom-bed –*
>
> *And shriek'd and started with affright,*
> *And upward, upward, sped and sped,*
> *For the carven angel was as cold as the dead.*
>
> *And the bar of heaven closes at night.*

I presume, since the angel was thirsty, that he went back for a drink, only to arrive too late for last orders. But, as with so much of Marzials's work, the ultimate meaning is obscure.

He sent a copy of the book to the poet and painter Dante Gabriel Rossetti, who replied that he had some 'difficulty in writing about it…'

> *I think Dowsabella much the most valuable poem in the book, but there are all the jarring points remaining in it. A great deal is disjointed – a great deal inconceivably forced or neglected in my judgment; yet it has something truly pastoral in a strange new way, and the tragic element is intense and memorable.*[5]

---

[5] That'll be the fennel, if you ask me.

> *I think you have made an unfortunate choice of a leading poem. The Gallery of Pigeons, besides the objection of its odd title, has almost less starting point, and labours perhaps more under a throng of (pardon again) puerile perversities in diction than any piece in the volume...*

Like the rest of us, he obviously couldn't pronounce 'Hyüeèps'. Rossetti liked some of the poems – he praises 'Gabrielle' for its 'crude power' – but he failed entirely to appreciate 'A Tragedy' and 'The Sun of my Songs', which he said 'appear to me to be written on a plan absolutely inadmissible...'

Marzials was greatly discouraged by this letter and complained quite rightly that

> *Rossetti does not seem to see (by what he picks out to admire) what I am driving at; he praises my imitations, and not the me, in the book.*

The Gallery of Pigeons was Marzials's only published collection of poetry. Instead, he turned his attention to songwriting, at which, surprisingly, he proved to be very good. He left the British Museum in 1882, and travelled on the continent. His only publication of this time was *Pan-Pipes*, a collection of traditional songs illustrated by the famous Victorian artist Walter Crane. Those who hoped for a musical version of *Dowsabella* will be disappointed, although the title page, with its topless nymph emerging from the reeds whilst a languid satyr toys with his pan-pipes, is eerily reminiscent of Dowsabella and her fennel.

In 1893 he returned to London where he submitted some pieces for *The Yellow Book*. He even attended the celebratory dinner on 15 April 1894, where he debated the merits of old ballads with W.B. Yeats.

The two poems published in *The Yellow Book* are not among his best, although 'To A Bunch of Lilac' contains the intriguing lines:

So full of ineffable Mearning,
So balmy, mystical, deep,
And faint beyond any discerning,
Like far-off voices in sleep –

I have no idea what 'Mearning' means. Perhaps it is a combination of meaning and yearning. Maybe he was yearning meaningfully, or possibly meaning something in a yearning sort of way. Or maybe he, like his readers, was just yearning for some kind of meaning.

His later life was not happy. He became addicted to chloral and in 1900 he appears to have suffered some form of breakdown. In 1911 Ford Madox Hueffer wrote that his career had been 'tragic', assuming he was now dead. In fact he was living in Devon, which, admittedly, amounts to the same thing. He retired to a farm in Colyton, where he supported himself by singing and teaching music. Living in one small room, he used to consume endless amounts of beetroot and play the piano on a hillside under the stars.

And that would be that, were it not for the fact that, while researching this genius, I stumbled across a manuscript written in his own hand, and containing a previously unpublished poem.

It is contained in a scrapbook of Marzials's memorabilia which he gave to his great friend Sir Edmund Gosse. There are two photos of the poet – looking suitably poetic with long flowing hair and resting his head on his arm – and some letters. And there is also a poem called 'The Poet and His Wanton Wit', which contains some of Marzials's finest verse.

I imagine the reason it never reached print was its subject matter. Because this is a risqué poem – a poem that unabashedly and openly uses the word 'fondling'. Lots of times. Lots and lots and *lots* of times. It starts with a long passage about a river meeting the sea:

Said the winding of the river
  To the waving of the sea:
'Let us fondle on forever
  I with thou and thou with me.'

Soon, however, the river grows sick of all this fondling and asks to be set free:

> ... *O Sea let love be over*
> > *For I'm a-wearying fast of thee*
> *Of salt and fondling love to lover*
> > *And all that once was sweet to me.*

But the sea refuses to let the river go, and they continue into eternity:

> *They fondle on, and on, and on*
> > *The sea with the river, the river the sea*
> *Waving a woundling[6] that never is done*
> > *Up to the edge of eternity.*

I've checked in the dictionary, but take it from me: there is no such word as 'woundle'. However, as I am now the acknowledged expert in Marzials studies I feel confident in defining it as 'the act of winding in a fondling manner'.

After this, the poem changes and, without a break, we are introduced to the Poet and his lover Kitty:

> *My mouth was made for kissing*
> > *Did Kitty cry to me*
> *My bosom heats for pressing*
> > *Its beauties out to thee*
> *Or taste me as an apple-fruit*
> > *That is so fair to see*
> *Or crush me as a citron shoot*
> > *That smells so savoury*
> *And toy with me which way you will*
> *For I must fondle me my fill*
> *And fondle, fondle, fondle still*
> > *Yet leave a-fondling time for thee[7]*

---

[6] The word was originally 'fondling' in the ms. But he'd obviously had enough of fondling by then, and had to invent a different word.

[7] OK, he obviously *hadn't* had enough of fondling.

Say what you like about Kitty, but it is a considerate gesture of her to leave enough a-fondling time for her lover. Especially when her bosoms have just been pressed. By now the reader is, I must admit, getting a bit tired of all this fondling, but Marzials is still going:

> And Oh! I found her savoury sweet
> > As never found a flower the bee
> Her face and throat and mouth and feet
> > And hair a-tangling knee to knee…

Personally I find this stanza rather worrying: she either has very long hair, or very hairy knees. Whatever the case, after this Kitty with her hairy limbs goes to sleep and the poet slips out to his day job. He appears to be some kind of minstrel, but instead of singing ordinary songs, he is unable to sing of anything but Kitty and 'how well she fondled me'. All that mingling has gone to his brain and the poem ends with the minstrel trapped in an endless round of woundling:

> And ever since along my soul
> The songs of Kitty surge and roll
> As river and sea from shore to shoal
> A-waving and winding two to a whole
> A-woundling a soul as it were to a soul
> That woundles on over God's great mole
> And sweeps where the waters and wastes of the soul
> With rushes that shriek from goal to goal
> As far as sight or thought can stroll
> > Lie waste and one awailing soul
> > > I' the torments of eternity.

It is a fine ending, although not without its difficulties. 'God's great mole' is not, as it might appear, an enormous burrowing mammal, but 'mole' as in 'harbour'. Although I admit that it still makes no sense. 'Rushes that streak from goal to goal' puts the reader in mind of a rather frantic football match, and does not sit happily with the rather relaxed image in the next line of 'sight and thought' taking a leisurely walk into the distance.

But who am I to question a genius? It is clear that this poem, with its incessant parade of steamy fondling and woundling its hairy knees and enormous moles, was too much for Marzials's public. And so it lay, undiscovered, for over a century.

I am proud to have played a small part in restoring it to the public's gaze, for it establishes Marzials as having written not only the worst tragic poem ever, but also the worst erotic poem ever written.

And it never mentioned fennel once.

Bibliography

Passionate Dowsabella (A Pastoral), London, 1872
The Gallery of Pigeons and Other Poems, London, 1873
Pan-Pipes, Routledge, London, 1883
Selected Poems of Theo Marzials, ed. John M. Munro,
    American University of Beirut, 1974

☞ Bosom Fanatics
George Wither; J. Gordon Coogler; Francis Saltus Saltus

☞ Falero-lero-loo, Riddlety-diddlety Poets
George Wither; Rev. William Cook; James Whitcomb Riley;
Rev. Edward Dalton

☞ Four Stars and Better
Margaret Cavendish; James McIntyre; Joseph Gwyer; Julia
Moore; William MacGonagall; Francis Saltus Saltus; Pedro
Carolino; Walter Reynolds; Shepherd M. Dugger; Amanda
McKittrick Ros

☞ Made-Up Words and Strange Syntax
'Lord' Timothy Dexter; Leopold John Manners De Michele;
Pedro Carolino; Nancy Luce; Amanda McKittrick Ros

****

Francis Saltus Saltus *(1849–89)*
The Wholesome Decadent

In Max Beerbohm's story *Enoch Soames*, he tells the tale of a failed poet of the so-called 'Decadent' school, who publishes small books of verse with titles like 'Fungoids' and 'Negation'. I can find no evidence that Beerbohm had actually read the works of Francis Saltus Saltus, but there is an uncanny likeness.[1]

Although he died when he was only thirty-nine, Francis Saltus Saltus[2] wrote over five thousand poems, in a style that can only be described as 'Decadence-by-numbers'. His portrait shows a young man with waxed moustaches, wearing a hat that is slightly too small for him. It is a telling image, for no matter how hard he tried to convince the reader of his decadence, it never quite seems to fit. However much he talked of drink and cigarettes and the pornographic bits in the Bible, he comes across as rather a cheerful young man. Here, for example, is his description of a spider. I am not sure what he means by 'dictatorial thighs', but the line about the 'leprous nudity of forsaken halls' is rather lovely:

> *Then all thy feculent majesty recalls*
> > *The nauseous mustiness of forsaken bowers*
> *The leprous nudity of forsaken halls –*
> > *The positive nastiness of sullied flowers.*

[1] Like Soames he has been shamefully forgotten. The copy of his book *The Bayadere and Other Sonnets* which I consulted in the Bodleian Library had none of its pages cut. I was the first person to read it.

[2] I don't know why he had two surnames, but one is reminded inescapably of the ex-General Secretary of the United Nations, Boutros Boutros Ghali.

> *And I mark the colors yellow and black*
> > *That fresco thy lithe, dictatorial thighs,*
> *I dream and wonder on my drunken back*
> > *How God could possibly have created flies!*[3]

The last line gives it away. No matter how decadent he was being, no matter that his back was, apparently, completely drunk, Francis always had time for a sunny smile and a joke. He was just too cheerful to be decadent for long. Nevertheless he does try. No one can accuse him of not trying to cram as many decadent elements into his poems as possible:

> *Oh! such a past can not be mute*
> > *Such bliss can not be crushed in sorrow,*
> *Although thou art a prostitute*
> > *And I am to be hanged tomorrow.*

His verse drama *Dolce Far Niente* shows a similar lack of conviction. It is set in Seville (so why it has an Italian title is anyone's guess) and tells the tale of Don Alonzo and his attempts to seduce Serafina. Don Alonzo has laid a cunning trap to ensure he is alone with his beloved:

> *DON ALONZO: Your duena, gagged, lies cursing us down stairs,*
> > *Your madre in the church is at her prayers;*
> *A forged letter, hem! but as you bid,*
> > *Now sends your noble padre to Madrid....*

Unfortunately it is very hot and Serafina is not keen to get all sticky:

---

[3] Compare this with Enoch Soames's poem 'To A Young Woman', which includes the lines

> Pale tunes, irresolute
> And traceries of old sounds
> Blown from a rotted flute
> Mingle with noise of cymbals rouged with rust.

It's an uncanny impersonation.

SERAFINA: *Charming indeed; considering the heat,*
  Your graceful Muse with Vega's could compete.
  But pray lie still, and calm such ardent fire,
  Love is not pretty when we both perspire...

In true decadent poetry, Don Alonzo would seduce and abandon Serafina, or possibly watch laughing while she threw herself from the balcony. In Francis's version they both decide just to have a nap.

DON ALONZO: *How sweet it is to slumber, cool and free,*
  I love you –
SERAFINA: *I adore you.*
BOTH: *Dream of me!*

(Both sleep.)

However, the poem does include the lovely lines

Her laugh is like sunshine, full of glee,
And her sweet breath smells like fresh-made tea.

Tea also features in his sonnet sequence *Flasks and Flagons*. The sequence was obviously meant to be a shocking celebration of alcohol, a debauched romp from absinthe to whisky to gin to Chartreuse vert. But Francis can't help himself, and right at the end he slips in verses about tea, coffee and chocolate. And though he makes strenuous efforts, it is hard to be decadent about cocoa:

Liquid delectable, I love thy brown
Deep-glimmering colour like a wood-nymph's tress;
Potent and swift to urge on Love's excess,
Thou wert most loved in the fair Aztec town
Where Cortes battling for Iberia's crown,
First found thee, and with rough and soldier guess,
Pronounced thy virtues of rare worthiness
And fit by Madrid's dames to gain renown...

His sonnet on tea is wonderfully overwritten:

> From what enchanted Eden came thy leaves
> That hide such subtle spirits of perfume?
> Did eyes preadamite first see the bloom,
> Luscious nepenthe[4] of the soul that grieves?

At times one wonders just what he has been slipping in his cuppa:

> Thy amber-tinted drops bring back to me
> Fantastic shapes of great Mongolian towers,
> Emblazoned banners, and the booming gong;
> I hear the sound of feast and revelry,
> And smell, far sweeter than the sweetest flowers,
> The kiosks of Pekin, fragrant of Oolong!

Francis always goes that bit too far. It starts promisingly but the subject cannot support the ludicrously over-inflated language. 'To a Scrap of Seaweed' shows this only too well:

> Tossed by a tempest and fluctuant tide
>   The vulgar plaything of the slimy eel;
> Crushed by the vessel's keel or cast aside,
>   What bitterness thy injured heart must feel!

Whatever suffering the seaweed has endured, however many eels may have played with it, the idea that it has become embittered is hard to believe.

Frequently, of course, the subject itself is stupid to start with. One of the key features of decadence, for example, was boredom – the terrible, crushing ennui of the end of the century. But his poem 'God's Ennui' somehow fails to convince:

> I am the Lord and Master over all;
> In me the essence of creation lies;
> ...
> But weary of my unquestioned powers I grow,
> Feeling at times that I could gladly see

[4] Nepenthe: a drink containing sedative properties. He was obviously confusing it with Horlicks.

> *The worlds I have created swoon and fade,*
> *Annihilated by a single blow;*
> *And then again I often long to be*
> *The lowliest worm that I have ever made!*

Try as I might, I just cannot imagine God being bored. Especially not when he sounds like a student who can't be bothered to get out of bed.

Pastels and Portraits is another sonnet sequence, this time celebrating historical figures. Most of these are emperors and kings, and, typically, Francis decides to take a rather perverse line. His defence of Caligula, for example, is just arguing for the sake of it:

> *Imbecile brute, monster of blood and crime,*
> *A revel of slaughter, infamy and pain,*
> *'Twas thy atrocious, grand and impious reign*
> *That soiled the laurels of Caesar in Rome's shrine.*
> *Yet what a marvellous festal life sublime!*
> *Oceans of gore did the arenas stain;*
> *With what Imperial pride thou didst disdain,*
> *In rapine, incest, lust, the Fates and Time!*
> *But history, in its calm impartial page,*
> *Has doomed thy deeds to an undying shame,*
> *But I, a dreamer, doubt the impeccable sage,*
> *And openly avow I love thy name...*

The main thought behind this poem appears to be, 'say what you like about Caligula, but at least he was keen on his work'. There are other joys to be found in this sequence, notably his lovely lines on Richard III:

> *Was not your hump enough to make you bad,*
> *Politic despot?*

And his poem on Queen Elizabeth I indicates that she had hidden depths:

> *Poor foolish virgin that foreswore Love's creeds*
> *While a warm harlot heart throbbed strong with lust...*

He goes on to celebrate poets such as Baudelaire, decadent heroes like the Marquis de Sade, and, strangely, the four Musketeers.

Another feature he shares with the poets of the late nineteenth century – especially the bad poets of the late nineteenth century – is an underlying eroticism. Or not so underlying, in Francis' case. His poem 'To Yulma' is feculent[5] with erotic imagery. I do not know for certain what Yani's minaret was, nor its precise dimensions, but it certainly casts an impressive shadow:

> *Like soft twin moons thy rounded bosoms gleam*
> *Veiled in the shade of Yani's minaret,*
> *And like an undulate tide of perfumed jet*
> *Thy sequin-studded tresses downward stream.*

In all this overblown imagery, it is easy to forget that Francis was a skilled rhymer as well. At his best he could produce rhymes as appalling as those of any bad writer:

> *Sad, on Broadway next afternoon,*
> *I strolled in listless manner,*
> *Humming her most detested tune,*
> *And smoking an Havana.*

In Beerbohm's story, Enoch Soames is that most unusual of people, a Catholic diabolist. There is a similar contradiction in Francis. He was a wholesome decadent. No matter how hard he tried to be bored, depressed and debauched he always cheered up in the end. He might have felt obliged to sip absinthe, but he really just wanted a nice cup of tea.

[5] Oh no, it's catching.

Bibliography

Honey and Gall, Philadelphia, 1873
Shadows and Ideals, Buffalo, 1890
The Witch of En-dor and other poems, Buffalo, 1891
Dreams After Sunset, Buffalo, 1892
Flasks and Flagons, Buffalo, 1892
The Bayadere and Other Sonnets, London, 1894
Fact and Fancy, New York, 1895

☞ Bosom Fanatics
George Wither; J. Gordon Coogler; Théophile Marzials

☞ Four Stars and Better
Margaret Cavendish; James McIntyre; Joseph Gwyer; Julia Moore; William MacGonagall; Théophile Marzials; Pedro Carolino; Walter Reynolds; Shepherd M. Dugger; Amanda McKittrick Ros

☞ Plays and Verse Drama
James Henry Powell; William Nathan Stedman; Walter Reynolds

☞ Unusual Subjects
Margaret Cavendish; Rev. Samuel Wesley; The Devout Salutationist; James Grainger; Rev. Cornelius Whur; James McIntyre; Solyman Brown; Nancy Luce

***

Nancy Luce (1811–90)
The Chicken Poet of New England

Nancy Luce's most famous poem celebrated two tragic deaths.

> Lines composed by Nancy Luce about poor little Ada Queetie and poor little Beauty Linna, both deceased. Poor little Ada Queetie died February 25th, Thursday night at 12 o'clock, aged most 9 years. Poor little Beauty Linna died January 18th, Tuesday night, most 2 o'clock, 1859, aged over 12 years. She lived 11 months lacking 7 days after poor sissy's decease.

It would take a heart of stone not to be moved by this introduction, and by the time we get to the medical details, tears are streaming down our faces:

> Poor little Ada Queetie's last sickness and death[1]
> Destroyed my health at an unknown rate,
> With my heart breaking and weeping,
> I kept the fire going night after night, to keep poor little dear warm,

After all this tragedy, it comes as something of a surprise to discover that the author is talking about her chickens. Ada Queetie and Beauty Linna were just two of the hens which Nancy tended with so much care on her farm in Martha's Vineyard.

> Poor little thing, she was sick one week
> With froth in her throat,
> Then 10 days and grew worse, with dropsy in her stomach,
> I kept getting up nights to see how she was.

[1] This seems to imply she had a previous sickness and death.

Never have hens been more cossetted. It was the chicken equivalent of intensive care.

Nancy was a true eccentric. She was a kind of livestock feminist: not only did she live alone, but all the animals on her farm were female. The chickens were, of course, her favourites, their habits observed with great fondness:

> When she used to be in her little box to lay pretty egg,
> She would peek up from under the chair.

she wrote, of Ada Queetie, or possibly Beauty Linna, or maybe another chicken entirely[2]. Whichever chicken it was, it proves they were truly free range.

Indeed, visitors who went to her farm to buy eggs found that they weren't just buying any eggs, these were limited edition eggs – each one inscribed by hand with the name of the chicken who produced it and the date it was laid. Now that's what I call quality control.

Her poetry is more akin to a kind of free-form meditation – although it cannot have come in a rush; her handwriting is a series of elaborate, almost ornamental letters. There is certainly no attempt to rhyme.

> She would do 34 wonderful cunning things,
> Poor sissy would do 39,
> They would do part of them without telling,
> And do all the rest with telling.

Yes, this woman could truly talk to the animals – well, the chickens at any rate.

In the only surviving picture of her she looks uncannily like Anthony Perkins 'mother' in Psycho. She is sitting in a rocking chair holding a pair of rather scrawny chickens. They may, for all I know, be Ada Queetie and Beauty Linna. They are certainly not looking well.

---

[2] She gave her chickens wonderful names. Along with Ada and Beauty she also had Levendy Ludandy and Fasheny Alome. They sound like the cast of an American daytime soap.

During her lifetime, both Martha's Vineyard and Nancy Luce became popular tourist attractions. Her first and only book of verses was printed in 1860 and she sold them at 25 cents a copy at the gate of her farm, making it possible to pick up some bad poetry and half a dozen eggs at the same time.'[3] She died in 1890 at the age of 79. Visitors can see her grave in the West Tisbury Cemetery, where it is lovingly tended by some of her admirers – who have thoughtfully placed nearby several model chickens and a few plastic eggs.

Bibliography

A Complete Edition of the Works of Nancy Luce, New Bedford, 1875

☞ Made Up Words and Strange Syntax
'Lord' Timothy Dexter ; Leopold John Manners De Michele; Théophile Marzials; Pedro Carolino; Amanda McKittrick Ros

☞ Unusual Subjects
Reverend Samuel Wesley; Margaret Cavendish; The Devout Salutationist; James Grainger; Rev. Cornelius Whur; James McIntyre; Solyman Brown; Francis Saltus Saltus

[3] Throw in a copy of Joseph Gwyer's verse and you could have some potatoes as well.

****

Julia Moore *(1847–1920)*
The Sweet Singer of Michigan

> *And now kind friends, what I have wrote,*
> *I hope you will pass o'er,*
> *And not criticize as some have done,*
> *Hitherto herebefore*
> from 'The Author's Early Life'

Julia A. Moore is America's greatest bad poet, and one of the small handful of all-time greats. Her work contains all that we require from a truly inept poet: bad rhymes, irregular metre, contorted grammar and small children dying like flies.

She was born Julia Davis in Plainfield, Michigan, in 1847. Although she had to manage the family and look after her invalid mother, she worked hard at school and soon began to write her first 'sentimental' songs, taking her subjects from the people who lived, worked and, apparently, died in bizarre circumstances all around her. 1876 saw the publication of her first book, *The Sweet Singer of Michigan*. It met with widespread praise. 'Shakespeare could he read it, would be glad that he was dead', said the *Rochester Democrat* in a piece of logic worthy of Julia herself.

Her poem 'Centennial' is one of the highlights of the collection:

> *In the year eighteen seventy-six,*
> *A Fourth of July celebration*
> *Was held in Grand Rapids city*
> *In honor to our nation.*
> *...*

The Centennial arch on Campau Place
Was the most principal feature;
It was a grand beautiful sight
To all human sensitive creatures...

Whether inhuman sensitive creatures or even human insensitive creatures enjoyed it, she doesn't say.

In 'The Author's Early Life', the reader is given a unique insight into the origins of this great artist:

I will write a sketch of my early life,
It will be of childhood day,
And all who chance to read it,
No criticism, pray.
...
In the days of my early childhood,
Kent county was quite wild,
Especially the towns I lived in
When I was a little child.
...
My heart was gay and happy,
This was ever in my mind,
There is better times a coming,
And I hope some day to find
Myself capable of composing.
It was by heart's delight,
To compose on a sentimental subject
If it came in my mind just right.

As well as detailing her own poetic development, she paints an intriguing picture of the sporting life of her town:

On a moonlight evening, in the month of May,
A number of young people were playing at croquet,
They mingled together, the bashful with the gay,
And had a pleasant time and chat, while playing at croquet.
CHORUS:
This play they call croquet, croquet,
This play they call croquet,

> *It is amusement for the young,*
> *This play they call croquet.*
> from 'Croquet By Moonlight'

And, surprisingly for those who thought America had never found true religion, she praises the local cricket team:

> *In Grand Rapids is a handsome club,*
> *Of men that cricket play,*
> *As fine a set of skillful men*
> *That can their skill display.*
> *They are the champions of the West,*
> *They think they are quite fine,*
> *They've won a hundred honors well;*
> *It is their most cunning design.*

There is a subtle criticism of the weight of some of the players:

> *And Mr. Follet is very brave,*
> *A lighter player than the rest,*
> *He got struck severe at the fair ground*
> *For which he took a rest.*

Whilst her lines about the unfortunate Mr Dennis end with a certain sense of anticlimax:

> *When Mr. Dennis does well play,*
> *His courage is full great,*
> *And accidents to him occur,*
> *But not much, though, of late.*
> from 'Grand Rapids Cricket Club'

She is at her finest, however, when she writes of death and disaster. It seems somehow to bring out the best in her. In 'Ashtabula Disaster' she writes:

> *Have you heard of the dreadful fate*
> *Of Mr. P.P. Bliss and wife?*
> *Of their death I will relate,*
> *And also others lost their life;*
> *Ashtabula Bridge disaster,*

> *Where so many people died*
> *Without a thought that destruction*
> *Would plunge them 'neath the wheel of tide.*

The 'wheel of tide' is an intriguing phrase, summoning up images of people being both run over by a train and drowned.[1] Meanwhile, 'Hiram Helsel' tells the tragic story of a fifteen-year-old boy who is stunted by 'malignant forces':

> *Once was a boy, age fifteen years,*
> *Hiram Helsel was his name,*
> *And he was sick two years or so;*
> *He has left this world of pain;*
> *...*
> *He was a small boy of his age,*
> *When he was five years or so*
> *Was shocked by lightning while to play*
> *And it caused him not to grow,*
> *...*
> *Now he is gone, Oh! let him rest;*
> *His soul has found a haven,*
> *For grief and woe ne'er enters there,*
> *In that place called heaven.*

Rhyming 'haven' with 'heaven' is rather inspired. In 'I Wonder Where My Papa Is?' disaster strikes the family of Lilly Long:

> *I wonder where my papa is,*
> *Oh, where could he have gone,*
> *I wonder why he does not come*
> *And see his Lilly Long.*
> *...*
> *No, he never would have left me*
> *And mamma without aid;*
> *I fear my papa has fallen*
> *A victim of the 'plague.'*

---

[1] Chernyshevsky would be proud. See p.173.

While 'Little Libbie' shows an early and prescient example of the dangers of eating beef. I may be reading too much into it, but the doctors don't sound as if they treated the matter with enough urgency. The phrase 'tried their skill awhile' hardly smacks of paramedics working at full speed:

> *While eating dinner, this dear little child*
> *Was choked on a piece of beef.*
> *Doctors came, tried their skill awhile,*
> *But none could give relief.*

Like many of her contemporaries, she was a keen supporter of temperance. Her poem 'Temperance Reform Clubs' begins:

> *Some enterprising people,*
> *In our cities and towns,*
> *Have gone to organizing clubs*
> *Of men that's fallen down...*

In case this should mislead the reader into thinking these clubs were just for the accident-prone, she explains the nature of their fall:

> *In estimation fallen low –*
> *Now they may rise again,*
> *And be respected citizens*
> *Throughout our native land.*

Julia is capable of springing a surprise on the unwary reader. 'Little Andrew', for example, tells of the boy's drowning:

> *Andrew was a little infant*
> *And his life was two years old.*
> *He was his parents' eldest boy,*
> *And he was drowned, I was told.*
> *On one bright and pleasant morning,*
> *His uncle thought it would be nice*

The reader knows what's coming: the boy is clearly going to fall through the ice. But no! It continues

To take his dear little nephew
Down to play upon a raft.

A stroke of genius.

One of my personal favourites – for obvious reasons – is 'The Brave Page Boys', which Julia tells us should be sung to the rather unpleasant-sounding tune of 'The Fierce Discharge':

John S. Page was the eldest son –
He went down south afar,
And enlisted in the Mechanics,
And served his time in the war.
Fernando Page the second son
Served in the Infantry;
He was wounded, lost both his feet
On duty at Yorktown siege.

Charles F. Page, she goes on, was killed 'in the fight of the Wilderness', whilst James B. Page served in the artillery. But it was young Enos Page who caused all the trouble. Aged only fourteen he ran away to join the army:

In Eight Michigan Cavalry
This boy he did enlist;
His life was almost despaired of,
On account of numerous fits,
Caused by drinking water poisoned –
Effects cannot outgrow...

The meaning of this last line is not clear, unless, like little Hiram Helsel, Enos has been stunted for life. Disaster, it is clear, can strike at any time. 'The Great Chicago Fire' begins cheerfully enough, but, as in one of Julia's poems, a painful experience is just around the corner:

In the year of 1871,
In October on the 8th,
The people in that City, then
Was full of life, and great.
...

> Some people were very wealthy
> On the morning of the 10th.
> But at the close of the evening,
> Was poor, but felt content,
> Glad to escape from harm with life
> With friends they loved so well,
> Some will try to gain more wisdom,
> By the sad sight they beheld.

In her preface, Julia claims that all her work is based on truth, which, if accurate, means that 19th-century Michigan was the most dangerous place on earth. Indeed, she introduces an entirely new concept of truth:

> This little book is composed of truthful pieces. All those which speak of being killed, died or drowned, are truthful songs; others are 'more truth than poetry.'

Experts are divided as to what she means by 'more truth than poetry'. Are her songs true or not? Indeed, are they poetry or not? Whatever the case, in her innocent delight in death, disaster and the stunting effects of lightning, she is just like many bad poets of the nineteenth century. In one way, however, she was different. What marks Julia out among her contemporaries is that she has a genuine self-awareness. She knows that people have been laughing at her.

> I wrote that little volume of poems without a thought of the future or what the public would think of me. I have found to my sorrow that the public thinks I am a fool. I was very foolish, I admit, in signing my original name to that little book, when a fictitious name would have done just as well. And another foolish act was when I told where I resided...

And there seems no reason to doubt her when she writes

> While writing the poems in that little book I never thought of the future or of fame... I wished for something different from all literary work, something to catch the public eye, and I think I have it in that little book. Its rare combination has caused a great many literary

people to laugh at my ignorance, yet at the same time, some of them could not help thinking that the sentiments were good, although so rarely constructed in poetry.

For that reason, Julia may be a ludicrous poet, but she is not a ludicrous person. She has too much dignity. She knows that her writing is not what defines her, despite what others might say.

After her second book, *A Few Words to the Public* in 1878, she published no more poetry. Maybe she stopped because of the discouraging criticism, or maybe because the book did not sell as well as the first. Or perhaps it was because she could no longer make the effort. She had a farm to run and a family to look after. And, after all, as she so memorably put it,

Literary is a work very difficult to do.

Bibliography

The Sentimental Song Book, Grand Rapids, 1876
A Few Choice Words to the Public, With New and Original Poems, Grand Rapids, 1878

☞ Death, Disaster and Disease
James Henry Powell; Eliza Cook; William MacGonagall; *Titanic* Poets; Amanda McKittrick Ros

☞ Four Stars and Better
Margaret Cavendish; James McIntyre; Joseph Gwyer; William MacGonagall; Francis Saltus Saltus; Théophile Marzials; Pedro Carolino; Walter Reynolds; Shepherd M. Dugger; Amanda McKittrick Ros

****

William MacGonagall (1825-1902)
The Worst British Poet

A year after Julia Moore published her first book, another gigantic talent burst into life on the other side of the Atlantic. In 1877 William Topaz MacGonagall, weaver and would-be actor, was inspired to write poetry.

> *I seemed to feel as it were a strange kind of feeling stealing over me, and remained so for about five minutes. A flame, as Lord Byron has said, seemed to kindle up my entire frame, along with a strong desire to write poetry; and I felt so happy, so happy, that I was inclined to dance...*

He tried at first to fight the desire, but fortunately for the history of literature, he failed:

> *It was so strong, I imagined a pen was in my right hand and a voice crying 'Write! Write!' So I said to myself, ruminating, let me see; what shall I write? then all at once a bright idea struck me to write about my best friend, the late Rev. George Gilfillan...*

The poem that followed was a masterpiece. MacGonagall called it 'the first poem I have composed under divine inspiration':

> *Rev. George Gilfillan of Dundee,*
> *There is none can you excel;*
> *You have boldly rejected the Confession of Faith,*
> *And defended your cause right well.*
> *The first time I heard him speak,*
> *'Twas in the Kinnaird Hall,*
> *Lecturing on the Garibaldi movement,*
> *As loud as he could bawl.*

This has all the classic elements of the great MacGonagall; the uneven line lengths, the accumulation of pointless detail and the ridiculously anti-climactic ending. Instead of showing the Rev. Gilfillan as a dignified man of learning, we are left with the picture of a bloke yelling his head off about Garibaldi.

Over subsequent years, MacGonagall was to write many verses which have cemented his reputation as Britain's worst poet. Perhaps his most famous works are his poems on the Tay Bridge. These four form a kind of tetralogy of badness, the 'bad poetry' equivalent of Eliot's *Four Quartets*. Together they take the reader through an emotional roller-coaster ride, as we experience the highs, the lows and then the highs again of the Tay and its tragically unstable railway bridges.

The cycle begins with the cheery optimism of 'The Address to the New Tay Bridge':

> *Beautiful Railway Bridge of the Silvery Tay!*
> *With your numerous arches and pillars in so grand array*
> *And your central girders, which seem to the eye*
> *To be almost towering to the sky.*
> *The greatest wonder of the day,*
> *And a great beautification to the River Tay,*
> *Most beautiful to be seen,*
> *Near by Dundee and the Magdalen Green.*
> *Beautiful Railway Bridge of the Silvery Tay!*
> *That has caused the Emperor of Brazil to leave*
> *His home far away, incognito in his dress,*
> *And view thee ere he passed along en route to Inverness.*

What the Emperor of Brazil was doing in Inverness is not known. Maybe he came for a game of golf. However, having firmly established the wonder of this bridge, the poet strikes a chill note of caution:

> *Beautiful Railway Bridge of the Silvery Tay!*
> *I hope that God will protect all passengers*
> *By night and by day,*
> *And that no accident will befall them while crossing*

The Bridge of the Silvery Tay,
For that would be most awful to be seen
Near by Dundee and the Magdalen Green.

It is a prescient thought. But for the moment all is well, and in the next poem, 'The Newport Railway', he sings of the company who are cashing in on the new bridge. His list of the dietary requirements of the Newport housewives is particularly fascinating:

Success to the Newport Railway,
Along the braes of the Silvery Tay,
And to Dundee straightway,
Across the Railway Bridge o' the Silvery Tay,
Which was opened on the 12th of May,
In the year of our Lord 1879,
Which will clear all expenses in a very short time
Because the thrifty housewives of Newport
To Dundee will often resort,
Which will be to them profit and sport,
By bringing cheap tea, bread, and jam,
And also some of Lipton's ham…

However, our delight at the shopping opportunities is short-lived. We have faced triumph, and now we must face disaster. Casting aside his grocery-fuelled optimism, MacGonagall takes up his pen in sadness to bring us the story of the Tay Bridge disaster:

Beautiful Railway Bridge of the Silv'ry Tay!
Alas! I am very sorry to say
That ninety lives have been taken away
On the last Sabbath day of 1879,
Which will be remember'd for a very long time.

The passengers' hearts 'were light and felt no sorrow' but they were fooling themselves. For by the time the train got halfway across, disaster struck:

> *So the train mov'd slowly along the Bridge of Tay,*
> *Until it was about midway,*
> *Then the central girders with a crash gave way,*
> *And down went the train and passengers into the Tay!*

The alarm is raised:

> *As soon as the catastrophe came to be known*
> *The alarm from mouth to mouth was blown,*
> *And the cry rang out all o'er the town,*
> *Good Heavens! the Tay Bridge is blown down,*
> *And a passenger train from Edinburgh,*
> *Which fill'd all the peoples hearts with sorrow,*
> *And made them for to turn pale,*
> *Because none of the passengers were sav'd to tell the tale...*

The rhyming of 'Edinburgh' with 'sorrow' is ambitious to say the least,[1] whilst the image of the alarm being passed from mouth to mouth is positively surreal. However, MacGonagall is not content to leave us with just the facts. Ever the prophet, he points to the unmistakable moral of the tale:

> *Oh! ill-fated Bridge of the Silv'ry Tay,*
> *I must now conclude my lay*
> *By telling the world fearlessly without the least dismay,*
> *That your central girders would not have given way,*
> *At least many sensible men do say,*
> *Had they been supported on each side with buttresses,*
> *At least many sensible men confesses,*
> *For the stronger we our houses do build,*
> *The less chance we have of being killed.*

[1] He repeats the same trick in his poem 'Edinburgh', which perfectly encapsulates the atmosphere of the summer festival:

> Edinburgh
> Beautiful city of Edinburgh!
> Where the tourist can drown his sorrow
> By viewing your monuments and statues fine
> During the lovely summer-time.

The final poem in the cycle, 'An Address to the New Tay Bridge', brings us back to the optimism of the first poems. And, in fact, to most of the lines from the first poem, for, faced with a new Tay Bridge poem to write, MacGonagall merely recycled a lot of the lines from the old one:

> Beautiful new railway bridge of the Silvery Tay,
> With your strong brick piers and buttresses in so grand array,
> And your thirteen central girders,[2] which seem to my eye
> Strong enough all windy storms to defy.

One feels he is tempting fate at this point.

> Thy structure to my eye seems strong and grand,
> And the workmanship most skilfully planned;
> And I hope the designers, Messrs. Barlow and Arrol, will prosper for many a day
> For erecting thee across the beautiful Tay.

Obviously 'Messrs. Bouche and Grothe', the engineers mentioned in the first poem, have been sacked.

One of the most remarkable passages is the description of the bridge's colour:

> And for beauty thou art most lovely to be seen
> As the train crosses o'er thee with her cloud of steam;
> And you look well, painted the colour of marone,
> And to find thy equal there is none...

This is a breathtaking piece of awfulness. Faced with the difficult prospect of finding a rhyme for 'none', he simply changes the spelling of 'maroon' to fit. Such a complete disregard for the English language is the mark of a true genius. Finally, he dismisses the bridge's only serious competition:

> The New Yorkers boast about their Brooklyn Bridge,
> But in comparison to thee it seems like a midge,

[2] As opposed to 'numerous arches' in the first poem. He had obviously been doing some research.

Because thou spannest the Silvery Tay
A mile and more longer I venture to say;
Besides the railway carriages are pulled across by a rope,
Therefore Brooklyn Bridge cannot with thee cope...

Some argue that this cycle should include a fifth poem, MacGonagall's famous lines on 'The Famous Tay Whale'. They assert that since the whale is in the silvery Tay, it should be included in the group. However, I am not inclined to include it with the others, on the grounds that (a) it does not contain a train (b) it does not contain a railway bridge and (c) it contains no mention of the Newport Railway Company, Messrs. Barlow and Arrol, Bouche and Grothe or the colour marone.

Nevertheless it is a wonderful poem, thrillingly conjuring up the might and magnificence of this fearsome beast:

So small boats were launched on the silvery Tay,
While the monster of the deep did sport and play.
Oh! it was a most fearful and beautiful sight,
To see it lashing the water with its tail all its might,
And making the water ascend like a shower of hail,
With one lash of its ugly and mighty tail.
Then the water did descend on the men in the boats,
Which wet their trousers and also their coats...

Eventually the whale was killed and put on display:

So Mr. John Wood has bought it for two hundred and twenty-six
pound,
And has brought it to Dundee all safe and all sound;
Which measures forty feet in length from the snout to the tail,
So I advise the people far and near to see it without fail.
Then hurrah! for the mighty monster whale,
Which has got seventeen feet four inches from tip to tip of a tail!
Which can be seen for a sixpence or a shilling,
That is to say, if the people all are willing.

The last line is, it must be admitted, a bit of a let-down, but perhaps MacGonagall was just being realistic about the prevailing economic conditions.

Like his contemporary Julia Moore he was much taken with death and disaster. Indeed, his book *More Poetic Gems* has something of a maritime disaster theme to it, with poems like 'The Albion Battleship Calamity', 'The Wreck of the Steamer "Stella"', 'The Wreck of the Steamer "Storm Queen"', 'The Wreck of the "Abercrombie Robertson"', 'The loss of the "Victoria"', 'the Burning of the Ship "Kent"' and 'the Wreck of the "Indian Chief"'. In all seven ships go down, eighteen individuals are commemorated (including Gladstone, Queen Victoria and a Little Match Girl), a theatre burns down, most of Scarborough goes up in flames and several thousand enemy soldiers and sailors are indiscriminately slaughtered.

One of his favourite poems – at least when it came to reciting it in public – was the ballad 'The Rattling Boy'. This stirring love poem contains a truly memorable chorus:

> *I'm a rattling boy from Dublin Town,*
> *I courted a girl called Biddy Brown,*
> *Her eyes they were as black as sloes,*
> *She had black hair and an aquiline nose.*
> *CHORUS*
> *Whack fal de da, fal de darelido,*
> *Whack fal de da, fal de darelay,*
> *Whack fal de da, fal de darelido,*
> *Whack fal de da, fal de darelay.*

MacGonagall's life was as eccentric as his poetry. He was born in Edinburgh in 1825[3] but moved to Dundee when he was young. A weaver by trade, he harboured secret ambitions to be an actor, and even acted himself in a remarkable

[1] He was always vague about his age, giving his birth date as either 1825 or 1830. To further confuse things, his wife, who could neither read nor write, gave his age on his death certificate as 62. This was in 1902, but MacGonagall himself said he was 62 in 1891, giving a birth date of 1829. So he could have been born in 1825, 1829, 1830 or 1840. It's your choice…

production of *Macbeth*. He had to pay the manager of the theatre for permission to appear, but the auditorium was packed
out:

> What a sight it was to see such a mass of people struggling to gain
> admission! hundreds failing to do so, and in the struggle numbers
> were trampled under foot, one man having lost one of his shoes in the
> scrimmage; others were carried bodily into the theatre along with the
> press.

As this was his big chance, he was determined to make the
most of it, so when it came to Macbeth's great death scene, he
made sure the fight with Duncan gave value for money:

> The actor who was playing MacDuff against my MacBeth tried to
> spoil me in the combat by telling me to cut it short, so as the audience,
> in his opinion, would say it was a poor combat, but I was too cute for
> him guessing his motive for it. I continued the combat until he was
> fairly exhausted, and until there was one old gentleman in the audi-
> ence cried out, 'Well done M'Gonagall! Walk into him!' And so I did
> until he was in a great rage, and stamped his foot, and cried out 'Fool!
> Why don't you fall?' And when I did fall the cry was 'M'Gonagall!
> M'Gonagall! Bring him out! Bring him out!' until I had to come
> before the curtain and receive an ovation from the audience.

In 1878 he walked from Dundee to Balmoral to crave an audience with the Queen, largely on the strength of a letter of
acceptance for one of his books of poems sent to him by the
Queen's secretary. After a long and arduous journey he
arrived at the gates of Balmoral, only to be told by the porter,
'Well, I've been up to the castle with your letter and the answer
I've got for you is they cannot be bothered with you.' He
protested that the porter was making it up, but had to leave
when the guard at the gate threatened to have him arrested.

It was like this all his life – he was a walking disaster area.
He even went to America to seek theatrical engagements.
Unfortunately he failed and had to wire a friend in Dundee
for the money to come home again. After he became a poet
he would give recitals to the public, but these inevitably

descended into chaos as students and hooligans pelted him with rotten vegetables. He was even banned from performing in Dundee because of the rowdy nature of his audience, provoking the plaintive appeal,

> *Fellow Citizens of Bonnie Dundee,*
> *Are ye aware how the magistrates have treated me?*
> *Nay, do not stare or make a fuss*
> *When I tell ye they have boycotted me from appearing in the royal Circus,*
> *Which in my opinion is a great shame,*
> *And a dishonour to the city's name.*

It is hard to read the accounts of MacGonagall and not feel sorry for him: he was the butt of so many jokes. Often he would see through them, but when it came to being asked to recite his poetry, he simply could not resist.

Few poets, good or bad, have suffered for their art as much as MacGonagall. But it has to be said that he brought much of the abuse on himself. MacGonagall was ridiculed because he was ridiculous. Towards the end of his life, for example, he took to styling himself William MacGonagall, Poet and Tragedian, Knight of the White Elephant, Burmah. The title, he believed, was bestowed on him by King Theebaw of the Andaman Islands, who 'failed to conceive how Rosebery could have been so blind as not to have offered to such a man as yourself the paltry and mean stipend attached to the position of Poet Laureate of Great Britain and Ireland'. Reading it now, it seems a transparent lie, yet he signed himself Sir William Topaz MacGonagall to the end of his life.

His story has an ending more tragic than any of his poems. He died in poverty, unaided by all those who had previously found him so amusing. The great MacGonagall, the finest bad poet of them all, was buried in a pauper's grave, his name spelt wrong on the death certificate.

Bibliography

Poetic Gems, Dundee, 1951
More Poetic Gems, Dundee, 1962
Last Poetic Gems, Dundee, 1968

MacGonagall's works were not collected until many years after his death. A complete edition is currently available.

☞ Death, Disaster and Disease

James Henry Powell; Eliza Cook; Julia Moore; *Titanic* Poets; Amanda McKittrick Ros

☞ Four Stars and Better

Margaret Cavendish; James McIntyre; Joseph Gwyer; Julia Moore; Francis Saltus Saltus; Théophile Marzials; Pedro Carolino; Walter Reynolds; Shepherd M. Dugger; Amanda McKittrick Ros

****

Joseph Gwyer (b. 1835)
The Penge Laureate

There were three main obstacles to Joseph Gwyer's self-appointed career as Poet Laureate. First, he was a potato salesman. Second, he lived in Penge. Third, he had all the poetic ability of one of his own tubers.

Nevertheless he pursued his career for many years, publishing several editions of his seminal work, *Sketches of the Life of Joseph Gwyer, (Potato Salesman) with his poems, (Commended by Royalty)*.

He was born in Wiltshire in 1835. During his early life he tried his hands at many careers. At one point he fell in with a rough crowd; however, he was saved from his dissolute ways by his conversion to Methodism and teetotalism. After a somewhat disaster-prone life (his autobiography is one long tale of failed businesses, dead and injured horses, arguments with relatives and tradesmen, and illness) he was 'divinely directed to the potato trade', in which career he spent the rest of his days.

Much as he loved his potato trade, what he really wanted to do was write. And in 1869 he found his inspiration, in the unlikely shape of Gladstone's Irish Church Bill. The poem 'A Review of the Past Four Years' gives us a breathtaking insight into the poet's life, from the abscess on his leg to the germs of his poetic talent:

> *The doctor gave me orders too,*
> *No more hard work I ought to do,*
> *So what to do I did not know,*
> *When poetry began to flow.*
> *The subject of my first attempt*
> *Was Irish church by Gladstone met,*

Since then many rhymes I've wrote
On subjects varied made a note.

'Irish church by Gladstone met' is a typical Gwyerism; all meaning has been sacrificed to make a rhyme which wasn't worth making in the first place. His first 'Royal' poem was a celebration of the marriage of the Duke of Edinburgh to Grand Duchess Marie Alexandrowna. It has similarly tortured syntax:

In works and charity and love,
The Duke as heretofore may prove,
And copy Albert, Prince the Good
His father gone, who highly stood.

One has to concentrate when reading Gwyer. A hasty reading might imply that he was talking about a good person called Albert Prince. His finest piece of mangled syntax occurs towards the end of the poem:

At evening too the dazzled light
Illumed the darkness of the night
I can't paint it for reasons best.
'Twas grand, though I in crowd was pressed.

He took copies of this poem to Windsor Park and sold several. 'In a few minutes I collected in this way upwards of a sovereign,' he writes. 'I also sold some potatoes which combined business with pleasure.'

From then on, every time he wrote a royal poem he sent it to the nobility. Naturally they responded, and their polite acknowledgements were collected and published in his books as 'commendations'. No matter how cool, he seems to have treated them all as if they were hearty recommendations. Here is a typically diplomatic example.

Dear Sir, – I have to acknowledge the receipt of a cheque for £1 towards the relief of the sufferers by fire at the Alexandra Palace, and also to express to you the Lord Mayor's thanks for your appropriate lines, which display a talent of a most uncommon order.

I am, dear Sir, yours &c., *JNO. R.S. VINE*
Private Secretary.

The state visit of the Shah of Persia gave him a chance not only to celebrate a grand event, but also to plug his views on alcohol:

> *The visit of the Shah of Persia here,*
> *To England, happy land and country dear,*
> *We welcome give to him and all who tread*
> *On Britain's soil, with plenty all are fed.*
>
> ...
>
> *The Shah did us a useful lesson teach,*
> *And this we trust the masses may reach,*
> *Intoxicating draughts he never does drink,*
> *If this we copied, should we not be better, think.*
> from 'On the Shah of Persia's Visit to England'

The opening line of his 'Visit of the Czar of Russia to England' induces a certain sense of *déjà vu* in the reader:

> *Welcome to the Czar of Russia here,*
> *To England's soil we love so dear,*
> *Our blessings best to him we give,*
> *And hope this union long may live.*
>
> ...
>
> *The Duke will show the Czar about,*
> *The nations greatness in and out;*
>
> ...
>
> *To Crystal Palace he will pay*
> *A visit on sixteenth of May,*
> *And as this stands so near our home,*
> *We shall contrive to see him come.*

I do hope he managed to see the Czar and maybe sell him some King Edwards. But it was not only the nobility that inspired his verse:

> *On Monday, July the 8th, at one,*
> *St. John's Sunday School children of Penge,*
> *United together and bent upon fun,*
> *So to Epsom went off for a change.*

...

It was a most happy and joyful meet,
On which I was pleased to look,
With Superintendents Crisford and Fleet,
Together with W.J. Crook.
from 'Sunday School Treat'

'The Magsman At London Bridge Outwitted' is one of his finest productions. In it he uses a freer and even less attractive poetic style to tell the story of a daring attempt at robbery:

'Twas on a Friday night, near ten o'clock, the fifth of May,
At the Railway Station, London Bridge, by Crystal Palace way,
I met an orange gent[1] in very flash array,
Who in the ticket lobby dropped his purse and turned away.

The honest Joseph gives back the purse and, by way of reward, is taken for a drink:

I said my pledge I never break and you the stuff should never take,
But if you like as I am a staunch teetotaller,
Instead of going to publichouse we will go to yonder coffee bar,
And have some tea, which I can drink with you,
And then I'll bid you each adieu.

Rhyming 'coffee bar' with 'teetotaller' is heady stuff, even by Gwyer's standards. The 'orange gent' tries to tell Gwyer that he can lend him money, if Gwyer will only put down a tiny deposit. But our intrepid potato salesman is not fooled. He alerts the police, and next day they arrest the man:

When they arrived at Stone End Police Station they turned the Squire's pockets about,
They found £2 and odd and other coins that did resemble gold,
Another thing I should have said was an India rubber screeching doll.

[1] As in 'someone from Northern Ireland'. I doubt the gent was actually coloured orange – it would have been rather conspicuous for a conman.

Gwyer's thirst for detail was never so apparent. What an 'India rubber screeching doll' is I have no idea, but it is the kind of true-life detail that makes Gwyer unique. Even though his verse is mainly drawn from life, he was capable of flights of fancy. His book also included a bizarre 'matrimonial map' which included places like the 'Vale of Gladness', the 'Land Of Bachelors and Spinsters' and the 'Domain of Petticoat Government'. The accompanying poem includes lines which show that he might not have been completely impervious to criticism:

> My first lines were on Gladstone and the great Bill Irish Church,[2]
> And now I am determined I will not be in the lurch,
> This matrimonial subject although quite out of my way,
> Yet I'll try hard that I may succeed on this very day.
> There are those London critics, too, who won't let me alone,
> Figaro, Punch and Judy, think my heart as hard as stone,
> And yet while they will print in their columns my name,
> I am joked along the street, 'tis a most terrible shame.

The poem, – and the map, – indicate that not all was entirely blissful in his own marriage.

> I have one of the best of wives, but we cannot see alike in the matter of my writings. Perhaps it is wisely ordained, as she knows something of the time, thought and expense it costs me to do it. I therefore have to write my simple lays and prose under great disadvantage, writing them mostly away from home, and many poems have been written in bed in the dark.

Personally I think the fact that he wrote many of his poems under the blankets in pitch darkness accounts for a lot. But he did not confine himself to poetry; the autobiographical and topographical sections of his book contain many gems for the lover of bad literature. Here, for example, are his impressions of Ramsgate:

[2] Bill Irish Church is probably a friend of Albert Prince the Good.

> *Truly at Ramsgate, Margate and surrounding neighbourhood there is most enchanting scenery, which must ever elicit the spontaneous throbbings of impulsive, sensitive natures like mine.*

He also wrote on burning political questions of the day, such as the method of ratepaying in south London. His political essay 'The Momentous Question' contains some stirring stuff in which he appears to be advocating self-rule for Penge:

> *Ratepayers! 'awake, arise or be forever fallen', shake off the yoke of thraldom already being rivetted around your necks like the collar on a saxon serf. Do not the districts of Penge, Anerley, Upper and South Norwood contain enough people to form a separate and distinct parish, with sufficient residents for a governing body?*

He put all his reviews, good or bad, in successive editions of his book. *The World* wrote:

> *Long have we watched in vain for the advent of a genuine new poet, but at last we have the unspeakable happiness of hailing that auspicious event … Until now this flower has been blooming comparatively unseen, and has been wasting its sweetness in the desert air of Penge and its vicinity. But the obscurity which has hitherto shrouded the lowly path of this gifted being must vanish before our quotation of his own touching and modest announcement that a copy of his poems 'can be had post free for seven stamps of the author, J. Gwyer, Potato Salesman, Penge Surrey. Also a sack of best potatoes forwarded to any part of London or country. Each sack of Potatoes can be tried before payment. Given with the first sack, without extra charge, a photograph of J.G.'s horse and van, mounted in a gilt frame.'*

The *New York Tribune* advised its young readers to take care:

> *To young people vibrating between poetry and potatoes, we unhesitatingly recommend the last-named commodity as by far the most profitable.*

It is a sentiment with which Gwyer would have agreed, for the book closes with a moving appeal from its author:

> *Our readers should all be aware that literary pursuits do not keep the wolf from the door. We therefore would suggest that should they require a certain vegetable that we deal in, viz.: – Potatoes, that all orders entrusted to us, will meet with our best attention and thanks.*

Gwyer, for all his literary ambition, never forgot that a poet must live. However lofty his poetic aims he never forgot his roots. Or, more correctly, his tubers.

Bibliography

Sketches of the Life of Joseph Gwyer, (Potato Salesman) with his poems, (Commended by Royalty), Ivy Cottage, Penge, 1877

☞ Four Stars and Better
Margaret Cavendish; James McIntyre; Julia Moore; William MacGonagall; Francis Saltus Saltus; Théophile Marzials; Pedro Carolino; Walter Reynolds; Shepherd M. Dugger; Amanda McKittrick Ros

☞ Poets of Royalty
Alfred Austin; Edward Edwin Foot

Nikolai Chernyshevsky (1828–99)
Revolutionary and Bad Novelist

Nikolai Chernyshevsky was a journalist and political philosopher and one of the most prominent influences on the Russian Revolution. More importantly, he was also an appalling novelist.

His only novel, *What Is To Be Done?*, was written whilst he was imprisoned and waiting to be deported to Siberia. The book was hugely influential, inspiring generations of Russians to live authentic lives, to cast off the shackles of conventionality and to set up their own sewing co-operatives. Lenin took it with him into exile, and even nicked the title for one of his own works. The orthodox view is that the book was a summary of Chernyshevsky's revolutionary ideas. My own opinion is that it was a magnificently subversive gesture against all literary institutions.

It opens with an apparent suicide – a traveller blows his brains out whilst standing on the parapet of a bridge, thus ingeniously combining two suicide methods for the price of one. We then travel to another city where the heroine, Véra Pávlovna, finds out about the suicide and believes that she and her partner are the cause of it. They decide to part.

After these two chapters, the author, flying in the face of tradition, inserts his preface:

> *Love is the subject of this novel; a young woman is its principal character.*
>
> *'So far so good, even though the novel should be bad,' says the feminine reader; and she is right.*

To which one is tempted to reply, 'No she isn't.' After this, the author decides to be brutally honest with his public:

> Yes, the very first pages of the tale reveal that I have a very poor opin-
> ion of the public. I have employed the ordinary trick of novelists. I
> have begun with dramatic scenes, taken from the middle or the end of
> my story, and have taken care to confuse and obscure them.

After which he promises, in effect, not to be interesting again:

> There will be no more mystery; you will be able to foresee twenty
> pages in advance the climax of each situation, and I will even tell you
> that all will end gaily amid wine and song.

He is determined to be honest and open with his readers,
even though some might be disappointed:

> I am an author without talent who doesn't even have a complete com-
> mand of his own language. But it matters little … because I have con-
> fessed that I have no trace of talent and that my novel will be faulty
> in the telling, do not conclude that I am inferior to the storytellers
> whom you accept and that this book is beneath their writings.

This, however, is a bit like a mugger telling you that he's not
very good at all that 'hitting' business. You still get mugged
– just less professionally. It doesn't matter that Chernyshevsky
is honest about his shortcomings. He is still bad.

The book restarts with a visit from Véra and her mother to
the opera. Then the scene switches to a café where, as far as I
can tell, a lady reveals that her bust is padded and bursts into
tears.

After this the plot settles down to tell the story of Véra,
and her elopement with Lopukhóv, a medical student spe-
cializing in the nervous system. Theirs is a pure relationship.
Indeed, at one point Véra's suspicious mother tests their
attachment by leaving them alone together. When she comes
to spy on them Véra is knitting a worsted waistcoat and
Lopukhóv is discussing the theory of self-interest. Between
them, the novelist tells us, is a distance of precisely two and
one-third feet. This chasteness continues into their marriage:

When they separate at night, she says: 'Good night my darling; sleep well!' Then they go, he to his room, she to hers, and there they read old books, and sometimes he writes.

True, the author does describe one steamy occasion where she goes to her husband's room to ask about the meaning of a sentence, but that's about as far as the ardour goes.

This night of passion is followed by some exciting chapters discussing the ins and outs of Véra's seamstress business and the profit-sharing scheme she devised. We are then introduced to a new character, Kirsánov – a man with 'an oblong face of rare whiteness'.

After this, things get complicated. Kirsánov loves Véra. Lopukhóv knows that Kirsánov loves Véra and, given that the relationship was based mainly around knitting and old books, heroically decides to give Véra up. But Véra is confused. Does she still love Lopukhóv? Or was she just in love with his theory of collective self-interest? Loputhóv kills himself, but whether he shot himself, jumped from a bridge, hanged himself with his own waistcoat or bored himself to death is not made clear.

Then, just when the reader is longing for the simplicity of a profit-sharing scheme, Rakhmétov appears. Rakhmétov is a real man. He lives a Spartan life, drinks no wine and sleeps on the floor. He 'will not touch a woman'. His head is not oblong, nor does he wear worsted waistcoats. He berates the others for their failings, and for putting the dress-making co-operative at risk. Then he leaves, never to appear in the book again.

After this, Véra decides to study medicine and she and Kirsánov have several fascinating conversations:

'My dear, I am reading Boccaccio … you are right in saying that he has very great talent. Some of his tales deserve to be placed beside the best dramas of Shakespeare for depth and delicacy of psychological analysis.'

'How do you like those humorous stories of his where he is somewhat impudent?'

'Some of them are funny, but generally they are tiresome, like every farce from being too coarse.'

As this chat is a bit too exciting, they move on to discuss the evils of tight clothes. Another heroine, Katerína, wanders in, apparently from another novel entirely, and the whole dreadful dirge ends in what one critic called 'a bewildering and incomprehensible Walpurgis night of Reason', plus the promise of a second part – alas never delivered.

The first, and as far as I can tell, the only translation into English was done by Benjamin R. Tucker in 1883. In his preface the translator tells us that

> This martyr-hero of the modern Revolution still languishes in a remote corner of that cheerless country, his health ruined and – if report be true – his mind shattered by his long solitude and enforced abstention from literary and revolutionary work...

Tragically, Chernyshevsky never recovered. He was released by the authorities but died in 1889. Although his book is badly written, creakingly plotted and peopled with characters that barely rise to two dimensions, let alone three, it had an immense effect on the Russian public and was read far more widely than Marx – showing that the public always prefer a fabulously bad book to a merely dull one.[1]

Chernyshevsky became a hero to Russians, and his book was required reading for all communist schoolchildren. Especially, one imagines, those in need of 'political re-education'.

Bibliography

What Is To Be Done?, New York, 1883

☞ Novels and Fiction
Margaret Cavendish; Shepherd M. Dugger; Amanda McKittrick Ros

---

[1] Of course, if Marx had added some young women and a few conversations about Boccaccio to *Das Kapital* he would have had a bigger readership.

****

James McIntyre (1827–1906)
The Great Canadian Cheese Poet

Fair Canada is our Theme,
Land of rich cheese, milk and cream.

When it comes to poetic celebrations of dairy produce there is only one name that springs to mind: James McIntyre.

Born in Scotland, McIntyre emigrated to Canada when he was fourteen. He became a furniture dealer and manufacturer in Ontario, first in St Catherines and then in Ingersoll. He had always dabbled in verse on a variety of themes, but it was at Ingersoll that he discovered the great theme of his work, the one subject that would guarantee his readers' full attention: cheese.

As he wrote in the preface to his *Poems of James McIntyre*:

We have written a number of dairy odes recently; these and our patri-
otic songs composed during the last year we trust will make the work
more interesting … As cheese making first began in this county and
it has already become the chief industry of many counties, it is no
insignificant theme.

He is absolutely right. There is nothing insignificant about McIntyre's poetry – it is a landmark in dairy-based literature.

What we might call McIntyre's Cheese Cycle[1] includes such poems as 'Lines Read at a Dairymaids' Social, 1887', 'Fertile Lands and Mammoth Cheese', 'Lines Read at a Dairymen's Supper', 'Father Ranney, the Cheese Pioneer' and 'Hints to Cheese Makers'.

[1] Or, as some experts call it, *The Dairyad*.

'Oxford Cheese Ode' begins with a robust challenge to those with preconceived ideas about Canada:

> The ancient poets ne'er did dream
> That Canada was land of cream,
> They ne'er imagined it could flow
> In this cold land of ice and snow,
> Where everything did solid freeze,
> They ne'er hoped or looked for cheese.

Personally I find this a little unjust. Most ancient poets never even knew about Canada, let alone scoffed at its cheese-making potential. Nevertheless, from this strong start, he goes on to produce a delightful image of a small vessel, afloat on a sea of dairy products:

> To us it is a glorious theme
> To sing of milk and curds and cream,
> Were it collected it could float
> On its bosom, a small steam boat...

Occasionally, his inspiration is such that he is vouchsafed a vision of the future. In his startling 'Prophecy of a Ten Ton Cheese' he dreams of a world where cheeses will shake free from all restraints:

> Who hath prophetic vision sees
> In future times a ten ton cheese,
> ....
> The greatest honour to our land
> Would be this orb of finest brand,
> Three hundred curd they would need squeeze
> For to make this mammoth cheese.

He has obviously thought out the details:

> But various curds must be combined
> And each factory their curd must grind,
> To blend harmonious in one
> This great cheese of mighty span,

And uniform in quality
A glorious reality.
....
To seek fresh conquests queen of cheese
She may sail across the seas,
Where she would meet reception grand
From the warm hearts in old England.

Perhaps the cynical reader doubts that old England would be too impressed were someone to foist a ten-ton block of Canadian cheddar on them. If so, they lack McIntyre's vision.

His first cheese ode, he tells us, was his poem about 'Father Ranney, the Cheese Pioneer':

When Father Ranney left the States,
In Canada to try the fates,
He settled down in Dereham,
Then no dairyman lived near him;
He was the first there to squeeze
His cow's milk into good cheese...

Father Ranney is the Leonardo da Vinci of cheese. A man ahead of his time in the dairy world.

He always took the first prize
Both for quality and size,
But many of his neighbors
Now profit by his labors,
And the ladies dress in silk
From the proceeds of the milk...

However, it is clear that his pioneering spirit has not spread to other dairy products:

But those who buy their butter,
How dear it is, they mutter.

McIntyre even wrote about silage, in a manner that would warm James Grainger's heart:

> *The farmers now should all adorn*
> *A few fields with sweet southern corn,*
> *It is luscious, thick and tall,*
> *The beauty of the fields in fall.*
> *For it doth make best ensilage,*
> *For those in dairying engage*
> *It makes the milk in streams to flow,*
> *Where dairymen have a good silo.*
> *The cow is a happy rover*
> *O'er the fields of blooming clover,*
> *Of it she is a fond lover,*
> *And it makes the milk pails run over.*
> from 'Ensilage'

However, like poetry, not everyone is given the gift of mammoth cheese-making:

> *In barren district you may meet*
> *Small fertile spot doth grow fine wheat,*
> *...*
> *But in conditions such as these*
> *You cannot make a mammoth cheese,*
> *Which will weigh eight thousand pounds,*
> *But where large fertile farms abounds.*
> *Big cheese is synonymous name,*
> *With the fertile district of the Thame,*
> *Here dairy system's understood,*
> *And they are made both large and good.*
> from 'Fertile Lands and Mammoth Cheese'

In 'Lines Read at a Dairymaids' Social, 1887' he is in a more sprightly mood, offering us two fine rhymes:

> *Throughout the world they do extol*
> *The fame of our town Ingersoll,*
> *The capital of dairyland,*
> *To-night it seems like fairy land,*
> *...*

Find some one now your heart to chear,
Thus celebrate the jubilee year,
Remember long this ladies' aid
And each bewitching dairymaid.

His greatest work, in the opinion of many poetry lovers,[2] is his 'Ode on the Mammoth Cheese'. Here he relates an experience that is every bit as epiphonal as Wordsworth's early morning walk on Westminster Bridge – the moment when he saw the biggest cheese of his life:

We have seen thee, queen of cheese,
Lying quietly at your ease,
Gently fanned by evening breeze,
Thy fair form no flies dare seize.
All gaily dressed soon you'll go
To the great Provincial show,
To be admired by many a beau
In the city of Toronto.

Inspired by the magnitude of the cheese, he leaps into new and daring rhymes:

May you not receive a scar as
We have heard that Mr. Harris
Intends to send you off as far as
The great world's show at Paris.

And thence into complete surrealism:

We'rt thou suspended from balloon,
You'd cast a shade even at noon,
Folks would think it was the moon
About to fall and crush them soon.

Not that he was exclusively cheese-oriented. 'Lines on Removal' advertises his new premises:

---

[2] Not to mention milkmen.

Come listen while we sound the lyre,
To announce the fact, that McIntyre
Is back again to his old block
And he has got a splendid stock.
...

His Furniture is cheap and good,
In every style and kind of wood
But none in health need 'e'er despair,
If they buy from him an easy chair.
When you his Warehouse then do seek,
'Tis where the brick bridge spans the creek.

and

The people all say and declare that it is true,
The best furniture is made of McIntyre's glue.

It must have been sticky to sit on.

Reactions to McIntyre's *Poems* were mixed, according to the notices he printed in his books. Colonel Denison, Toronto's police magistrate, 'found many interesting pieces on Canadian subjects in the volume' whilst someone called The Hon. Oliver Mowat was 'pleased with the patriotic spirit displayed in the poems'. Mr William Murray of Hamilton, however, was moved to verse:

In writing you do not pretend
With Tennysonian themes to blend,
It is an independent style
Begotten on Canadian soil.

It is a shame that Mr Murray did not publish himself, for he shows great promise. All that was needed, one suspects, was the right theme to drive him on, the one subject to propel his muse.

Perhaps he just needed some yoghurt.

Bibliography

Musings on the Banks of Canadian Thames, Ingersoll, 1884
Poems of James McIntyre, Ingersoll, 1889

☞ Four Stars and Better

Margaret Cavendish; Joseph Gwyer; Julia Moore; William MacGonagall; Francis Saltus Saltus; Théophile Marzials; Pedro Carolino; Walter Reynolds; Shepherd M. Dugger; Amanda McKittrick Ros

☞ Unusual Subjects

Margaret Cavendish; Rev. Samuel Wesley; The Devout Salutationist; James Grainger; Rev. Cornelius Whur; Solyman Brown; Francis Saltus Saltus; Nancy Luce

**

Bloodgood H. Cutter (b. 1817)
The Long Island Farmer

In 1867 the celebrated writer Mark Twain travelled to the Holy Land on board the steamship *Quaker City* on a journey he was to immortalize in his book *The Innocents Abroad*. Among the passengers on the ship was a poet, a man whom Twain dubbed 'Lariat'. 'The laureate of the ship is not popular,' wrote Twain, telling of how he wrote poems on every occasion and forced them on anyone in sight.

That man was Bloodgood Haviland Cutter,[1] a farmer from Long Island. He obviously bore no grudge, since twenty years later the title page of his book, *The Long Island Farmer's Poems*, carried the phrase 'Mark Twain's "Lariat" in "Innocents Abroad"' and an engraving of Twain.

Cutter's own observations on Twain are an indication of just how irritating his poems could be. It is one thing to be able to read his poems at leisure, it must have been quite another thing to be trapped with him on board a ship:

> *One droll passenger there was on board,*
> *The passengers called him 'Mark Twain;'*
> *He'd talk and write all sort of stuff,*
> *In his queer way, would it explain.*

Bloodgood was born at Little Neck, Long Island, in 1817. He acquired 'a limited education' at a small district school at Lakeville, but was kept home during the summer months due to his grandfather's somewhat restricted view of the value of school versus the value of getting the harvest in. In

---

[1] He got his unusual name from his mother, whose maiden name was Mary Bloodgood.

1840 he married Emeline Allen, a marriage which, according to Cutter, 'has glided along peacefully and happily in the main, with, perhaps now and then, a cloud of sorrow, with its silver lining'. He was probably talking about his poetry, for on page seven there is an engraving of his wife, looking somewhat resigned and accompanied by the verse:

> This is a likeness of my wife,
> The last part of her mortal life;
> Emeline Allen was her name
> Before our marriage changed the same.

In 1844 his grandfather died and Bloodgood inherited the Prospect Hill Farm, which 'commands a view of Little Neck bay, Fort Schuyler, and Willets Point fortification, almost equal to the Bay of Naples'. According to one biographer, he went on to cram the house full of over eight thousand books (including more than two hundred Bibles) as well as countless stuffed animals, waistcoats of all colours, antiques and guns of all descriptions. At his death the sale of his estate amounted to $900,662.95, most of which went to the American Bible Society.

He published his collected poems in 1886, when he was nearly seventy. Much of the book is taken up with the poetry written during his voyage on the *Quaker City*. He makes it clear that he nearly didn't make the trip:

> For months the papers did announce
> There would be an excursion grand,
> To start about the first of June
> On a voyage to the Holy Land.
> Many inducements were held out –
> To join them then I was inclined;
> But when the time did come to start
> I felt gloomy and changed my mind.

Such, alas, is the poetic temperament. Fortunately for lovers of bad writing, however, the ship was kept back by storms and Bloodgood changed his mind. The rest, as they say, is poetry.

> On Monday it began to clear,
> So I to New York city went,
> If the Quaker City had not sailed
> To go, I then was really bent.

At stanza seventeen the rhyme scheme changes, and one feels a strange sense of impending doom:

> We're on the Atlantic Ocean
> And I feel a strange commotion;
> Our ship doth ride the briny swell
> And does perform her duty well.
> Yet still when she does plunge and reel
> Sometimes makes me quite qualmish feel;
> Then I rush up to the vessel's side,
> And heave up in the briny tide.

Unlike many a lesser poet, Bloodgood doesn't just describe the sickness, he makes you feel sick as well.

Throughout the voyage he wrote poetry for the edification of the travellers. But he was not merely an artist; he was a natural philosopher as well. I was particularly taken with his theory about flying fish:

> For my own part I really think
> 'Twixt fish and birds it is a link;
> Like as between a bird and rat
> In that case is centered in a bat.

The voyage, like Bloodgood's poetry, was hard going. At Naples and Athens the ship encountered quarantine problems, and tragically for the history of Greek culture, Bloodgood was unable to visit Greece and recite his poetry on the Acropolis.

After a while the Americans on the ship began to get angry, and at Odessa the Russians rather unwisely provoked a mass outbreak of pouting:

> *Our passports were demanded then,*
> *And soon each one was handed out;*
> *But we, as the true Yankee men,*
> *Began at once at that to pout.*

I have never seen a lot of Americans pouting in unison, but I imagine it must be a fearsome sight. In the end, after some more pouting and a few hundred more lines of bad verse, they reached the Holy Land. Among the holy relics he found there, Bloodgood celebrates the blessed tomato of Gethsemane:

> *To thank you now I really ought,*
> *For the tomato that you brought,*
> *from the garden of Gethsemane,*
> *Where our blessed Lord did pray.*
> *...*
> *And then by picking out its seed*
> *You still performed a nobler deed,*
> *And when you get that to your home*
> *Tell them from Gethsemane it come.*
>
> from 'To Mrs. Dr. Gibson,
> on receiving a slice of tomato
> brought by her from the garden of Gethsemane'

He seems to have found the experience moving in every way:

> *And in the Dead Sea, as I stood,*
> *So warm it seemed to heat my blood;*
> *tasting the same, 'twas awful too,*
> *So nauseous I did out it spue.*

At 137 pages, some critics feel that 'The Voyage of the Quaker City' is too long, and indeed there are times when reading it that one feels it would be quicker and easier to take the journey.

His later poems are mercifully brief. The 'Address before the Queens Country Agricultural Society' returns us to a familiar topic of bad poetry – manure:

> But stick to the old fashioned plan,
> And try to do the best they can;
> That is plow deep, and manure well,
> In due time that will surely tell.

And here is a heartfelt plea on the eve of civil war:

> My brethren of chivalrous South Carolina
> A few words in kindness to you will I say,
> And advise you to consider well (indeed)
> Ere you determine, from this Union to secede.
> from 'To His Southern Brethren'

Personally I would have thought that the presence of a poet like Bloodgood in the North was virtually certain to lead to a split, if only to get away from him. Fortunately for America, he spent long periods abroad.

In 1884 he visited Britain, where once more his poetic talents burst forth. Here he is in the Tower of London:

> The edge of the axe seemed very thick,
> The sight of that would make some sick;
> In thinking what that axe has done,
> It does affect most everyone.
> We saw the crown and jewels rare,
> That are guarded with the greatest care;
> The famous Diamond Korinoor,
> With the other things I there did view.

I have tried and tried, but I can't see any way in which 'Korinoor'[2] rhymes with 'view'.

The trip seems to have been full of 'thoughts'. Westminster Abbey brought forth the 'Lines Composed Sitting on A Tomb':

> As I walked through with silent tread,
> O'er the tombs of their noble dead;
> Many thoughts of a solemn kind,
> Did very much impress my mind.

---

[2] He even got the name wrong. It should be Koh-i-noor.

Naturally, a talent like Bloodgood's was bound to attract fans, and his book contains correspondence with a Phebe Robinson, who requested the poet to write some verses commemorating her dead husband. Impressed by the verses, Phebe decided to devote herself to the care of the sick soldiers at the New York hospital, but

> the scenes there she witnessed, acting upon her highly nervous organisation, completely prostrated her physically and mentally… At times her mind seems to be entirely gone and when she returns to a sane condition, she frequently speaks of you, and desires her friends to read over to her several small poems which she had received from you.

Frankly I think the writer was being optimistic of a recovery; the desire to hear Bloodgood's poetry is hardly the sign of a return to sanity, if you ask me. To aid her recuperation, Bloodgood sent some more verses but within two pages we find him writing 'To the Memory of Mrs. Phebe Robinson'. The strain of his muse was obviously too much for her fragile mind – a warning perhaps to all those of a nervous temperament to read poets like Bloodgood H. Cutter with special care.

Bibliography

The Long Island Farmer's Poems, New York, 1886

☞ Tales of Travel
Thomas Costley; Pedro Carolino; Shepherd M. Dugger; Frederick James Johnston-Smith

Momentary Lapses

One of the criteria of a truly bad poet is consistency. To be admitted into the hall of fame one must have produced a solid body of work, not just the odd line. However, it is always instructive and enchanting when otherwise good poets – even great poets – suddenly slip up. Here is a brief selection from the works of rather boringly good writers showing what they could have achieved, if only they'd set their minds to it.

> *Up to battle! Sons of Suli*
> *Up, and do your duty duly!*
> *There the wall – and there the moat is:*
> *Bouwah! Bouwah! Suliotes,*
> *There is booty – there is beauty!*
> *Up my boys and do your duty!*
> Lord Byron, 'Song to the Suliotes'

> *When longer yet dank death had wormed*
> *The brain wherein the style had germed*
> *From Gloucester church it flew afar*
> *The style called perpendicular*
> *To Winton and to Westminster*
> *It ranged and grew still beautifuller...*
> Thomas Hardy, 'The Abbey Mason'

Wordsworth is particularly rich. If he'd stopped wittering on about daffodils he might have actually rivalled MacGonagall:

> *Spade! With which Wilkinson hath tilled his lands...*
> from 'To The Spade of a Friend'

This piteous news so much it shocked her,
She quite forgot to send the Doctor.
from 'The Idiot Boy'

His poem 'Goody Blake and Harry Gill' could have been written by Julia Moore:

Oh what's the matter? what's the matter?
What is 't that ails young Harry Gill?
That evermore his teeth they chatter,
Chatter, chatter, chatter still…

In March, December and in July,
'Tis all the same with Harry Gill;
The neighbours tell, and tell you truly,
His teeth they chatter, chatter still.
At night, at morning, and at noon,
'Tis all the same with Harry Gill;
Beneath the sun, beneath the moon,
His teeth they chatter, chatter still.

The mystic Henry Vaughan shows what happens when a word changes its meaning over the years:

How bright a prospect is a bright backside!

George Crabbe illustrates how easily the eyes can deceive us:

Grave Jonas Kindred, Sybil Kindred's sire,
Was six feet high, and look'd six inches higher.
from 'The Frank Courtship'

While Ruskin speaks to his heart sternly, but affection-
ately:

> *Thou little bounder, rest.*

John Gray seems to imply that the baby Jesus is sharing
the ox's meal:

> *The holy night that Christ was born*
>   *The ox stood reverently apart,*
> *Both ruminating eaten corn,*
>   *And pondering within his heart.*
> John Gray

While Richard Le Gallienne's poem 'R.L.S., An Elegy'
contains two memorable images:

> *The floating call of the cuckoo*
> *Soft little globes of bosom-shaped sound,*
> *Came and went at the window...*
>
> *...Then a lark staggered singing by*
> *Up his shining ladder of dew,*
> *And the airs of dawn walked softly about the room...*

'Bosom-shaped sound' speaks for itself, but the picture of
a lark, staggering up a ladder like a drunken window
cleaner, is delightful.

*

J.B. Smiley *(1864–1903)*
The Kalamazoo Poet

The Kalamazoo poet is a figure of mystery to me. He wrote two books of poems, *A Basket of Chips* and *Meditations of Samuel Wilkins*, which celebrate his part of Michigan in a unique manner.

'Beautiful Spring' starts off in a charmingly rural mode, but when we get to confused chickens and scratched horses it takes on a more mysterious note:

> The north winds are still and the blizzards at rest,
> All in the beautiful spring.
> The dear little robins are building their nests,
> All in the beautiful spring.
> The tramp appears and for lodging begs,
> The old hen setteth on turkey eggs,
> And the horse has scratches in all four legs,
> All in the beautiful spring.

Who, one wonders, has been scratching the horse? Is there a small person roaming the district, armed with sandpaper and a grudge against all things equine?

Meanwhile, 'Kalamazoo' contains an intriguing look at the mental health provision in the area during the late nineteenth century:

> The Michigan Insane Asylum
> Is up on the top of the hill,
> And some irresponsible crazies
> Meander around there at will.

This is hardly reassuring for the residents, and, as the poem continues, the reader is left unconvinced by the optimism of J.B. Smiley.

> *And they frequently talk to a stranger,*
> *And they sometimes escape, it is true,*
> *But the folks are not all of them crazy*
> *Who hail from Kalamazoo.*

And that is all I have discovered. Like some ancient codex, or long-lost papyrus, all we have are fragments.

Perhaps some intrepid American researcher would be willing to take up the search, to excavate more fragments of Smiley's verse.

On second thoughts, maybe we had best leave well alone.

Bibliography

Meditations of Samuel Wilkins, Kalamazoo, 1886
A Basket of Chips, Kalamazoo, 1888

Pownoll Toker Williams (fl. 1889)
A Sensitive Man

*P*ictoris Otia, *Poems* by Pownoll Toker Williams, MA, is a charming little book, lovingly produced with a title page designed by the author.

About the author himself, we know next to nothing. He was obviously a cultured man, for many of the poems have titles in Greek. He travelled a lot, particularly in Europe. And he wrote some charmingly bad verse. His 'Lines Written On The Lake Of Bourget By A Sensitive Man' begins:

> O Muse of poetry, who didst erewhile
> inspire the gentle Soul of Lamartine
> Please tell me what to say, and how to say it;
> I'm going to try and sing the lake at Aix.
> We went there in a two-horsed Omnibus,
> With ladies hampers and some other friends.

Alas, the journey is hampered by the presence of a demon musician:

> We drove some twenty minutes out of Aix
> Through a straight Avenue of shady trees;
> And one there was who would beguile the way
> By playing Tunes to luckless passers-by,
> To reassure them that he meant less harm
> Than e'en his Air suggested – or he thought
> To teach them what he knew of music; but
> He conceived music as a blatant noise.

We do not know what this hateful noise is, until we reach the very shoreline itself:

> *At the lake shore, the poet stands*
> *Here, may the Senses drink long draughts, subdued*
> *To silent Exstacy [sic] – Ah hateful strains!*
> *He's playing something out of Offenbach!*

The rest of the collection does not live down to this standard, although the poem entitled 'ΑΥΠΝΟΣ ΑΥΠΝΟΣ'[1] movingly embodies the problems of hot bed-linen:

> *Awake and not yet four! methought I slept.*
> *How hard and hot this pillow!*

And there is a poem called 'A Love Passage on the Lake of Hallstadt' which sounds exciting. But isn't.

Bibliography

Pictoris Otia, Poems, London, 1889

☞ Minor Victorians
Eliza Cook; Stephen Fawcett; Leopold John Manners De Michele; Alfred Austin; J. Stanyan Bigg

---

[1] Greek for 'Who set fire to this bed?'

Shepherd M. Dugger (fl. 1854–1938)
The Baedeker of Balsam Grove

On the whole, the modern travel writer has two choices. He can write a factual travel guide, or he can write a book recounting his adventures and experiences. It is *The Rough Guide to France* versus *A Year in Provence*. The truly bad travel writer, however, has a third way. He can write a factual guide wrapped within a wild romance and combine it all with poetry, statistical information and personal recollection. Or at least he can if he is Shepherd M. Dugger and the book is *The Balsam Groves of the Grandfather Mountain*.

Shepherd Monroe Dugger was a resident of Watauga County, North Carolina, where he worked as a superintendent of schools, a surveyor and engineer. Given such a background, the reader might expect *The Balsam Groves* to be dry and factual. Instead it reads as if Barbara Cartland was writing the Michelin Guide. The dedication runs:

> To the Lovers of
> THE SUBLIME AND BEAUTIFUL
> And Especially Those Who Have Grasped My Mountain Palm[1]
> This Book Is Dedicated.
> THE AUTHOR

Far from settling for mere description, Shepherd begins his work with a romantic story featuring an Episcopalian minister, a beautiful young lady and a gentleman called Leathershine who has been expelled 'from an institution of learning in the eastern part of the state'.

---

[1] He means his hand, and not a species of mountain plant.

The story opens on a July evening in 1860,

when Sol was shooting his last golden arrows across the mountain-tops from his rosy couch beyond the horizon…

Which gives a warning as to the kind of writing we can expect. The heroine, Lidie Meaks, is described as

a medium-sized, elegant figure, wearing a neatly fitted travelling dress of black alpaca. Her raven black hair, copious both in length and volume and figured like a deep river rippled by the wind, was parted in the centre and combed smoothly down, ornamenting her pink temples with a flowing tracery that passed round to its modillion windings on a graceful crown. Her mouth was set with pearls adorned with elastic rubies and tuned with minstrel lays, while her nose gracefully concealed its umbrage, and her eyes imparted a radiant glow to the azure of the sky.

I have looked up 'modillion' in the dictionary, but it is unhelpfully defined as 'a projecting bracket placed in series under the corona of the cornice in Corinthian, Composite and Roman Ionic orders', all of which makes Lidie's face seem rather architectural. 'Elastic rubies' is an interesting image, conjuring up a surreal world of stretchy gemstones rather than her lips, to which he is, I think, referring. 'Umbrage' means either 'shade' or 'disfavour', and I am not sure which is right in this case. Either her nose had small areas of concealed shade, or she was somehow using it to hide her disapproval.

On their first night they stay in a small hut, where we are introduced to Tom Toddy and his family and a hunter with the amazing name of Rollingbumb. The next day they start their ride up the mountain, allowing the author subtly to insert necessary facts about the region, such as

From the base of this cliff gushes and sparkles the coldest perennial spring isolated from perpetual snow in the United States. Its highest temperature is forty-two degrees, and half a pint from its unpolluted channel quenches the greatest thirst created by an exhaustive climb.

Whilst enjoying this forty-two-degree stream, they are joined by two other travellers, an event which causes Lidie some emotional upheaval:

> the beautiful rhododendron bloom that embossed her bosom now rose and fell with a deep sigh that pushed forward the elegantly rounded prospect behind it.

Something tells me that Shepherd M. Dugger has spent a bit too long on his own in the mountains. But Lidie's embossed bosom is heaving because the hero has arrived, in the shape of Charlie Clippersteel. Charlie reveals that, smitten by the presence of Lidie and her enormous rhododendrons, his icy regions are beginning to thaw:

> 'Pardon me, my friend,' said he: 'it cost me four years in a foreign land to travel to the frigid zone of my heart, where the snows that ended the summer of love were lighted only by the flitting meteors of the borealis race. But your unexpected presence here today, which I could not avoid, has placed that icy region again under the burning sun of the tropics... Let me drink and water a desert that will soon flourish with the green bay-tree and the balm of Gilead.'
>
> 'O God,' she cried, 'pardon the weakness of woman,' and burying her face in her bosom, her lachrymal lakes overflowed his garments with drops that were to him the myrrh of the soul.

After that, they wander about picking flowers such as 'ferns, pinks and the little evergreen shrub, Leiophyllum buxifolium'.

They decide that, since they have an Episcopalian minister handy, they will get married in the mountains. However, the wedding (which is also attended by a visiting band of moun-taineers) is interrupted by Leathershine, who claims that Lidie is engaged to him. Unsurprisingly, she falls to the ground in a dead faint.

It is clear that this is a vile calumny, and precisely the kind of thing that gets a man expelled from educational institu-tions. Clippersteel chases Leathershine off with a gun, Lidie is revived with the aid of brandy, and our hero takes posses-sion of his wife, flowery bosom, lachrymal lakes and all.

After this the book changes into what purports to be a simple guide book, but once a man has started calling the sun 'Sol' and lips 'elastic rubies' he is too far down that road to easily turn back. He describes inns and hotels in a wealth of detail:

> the floors in Eseeola Inn being as hard as lignumvitae and as slick as a peeled onion furnish the finest facilities for tripping the fantastic toe.
>
> Three thousand years ago Solomon said: 'There is nothing new under the sun'; but if he could come back and engage board at Eseeola Inn, he would find that something new has been invented; for he could holla 'hello' in a telephone and receive an answer from a social-minded fellow in the telephone office over at Cranberry, and he could chalk his cue and try his luck on a billiard-ball, like which no rotary object ever revolutionized across a rectangular game-table in the city of Jerusalem.

The idea of King Solomon calling his friends before a leisurely game of billiards is appealing. He would enjoy the food as well:

> Such is the variety and flavor of the food that, when you place your foot on the threshold of the masticating department, your nasal proboscis is greeted with the aroma of roasted mutton or beef, and the alimentary pupils of your orbicular instruments are fixed upon large slabs of comb honey, consisting of the gathered sweets from mountain flowers, and rivalling in delicacy the nectar of the gods.

Shepherd is justifiably proud of his land:

> The great Appian Way, leading from Rome by way of Naples to Brundusium, was probably not more interesting than the Yonahlossee Road…

Shepherd even displays a talent for bad poetry, although it is nowhere near as flowery as his prose style. 'The Lone Chimney' begins in sombre fashion:

> A lone Chimney stood in the valley,
> It had a sad story to tell;
> Of the children that warmed by its fires,
> And the house wherein they dwelled.
> ...
> Billy slipped out and played in the snow,
> In spite of his mother's alarms;
> He took the croup, he struggled for breath,
> And died in his mother's arms.

In a rather beautiful and striking meditation the poet declares that bits of decomposed humans are floating about all over the place:

> Our chemical elements fully set free,
> That rise from our dust to the air;
> Absorbed by the flowers, may color the rose,
> That's worn in the ladies' hair.
> ...
> These elements building in human food,
> In a maiden's blood may blend;
> And a young man kissing his sweetheart's cheek,
> May kiss a departed friend.

Whilst in the poem 'Sunnalee' the reader is left to wonder what exactly Jeahue English has been eating to make him so greasy:

> Rare Sunnalee, your breezes sweet,
> At noon from heat distinguish,
> While in yon field the sun does broil,
> The grease from Jeahue English.

Other elements of the book are disappointingly dry. However, even the rather statistical list of mountains has its high points, so to speak. I was struck with some of the names, particularly 'Tompkins' Knob' which apparently rises to 4,055 feet. The local tourist board should surely take note. T-shirts with 'I've been up Tompkins' Knob' are a guaranteed best seller.

His book attracted a considerable amount of attention, but unfortunately later editions did not help the narrative part at all. The freshness is gone. Lidie is referred to as 'Miss Lydia', and a man named Bodenhamer interrupts the action to discuss geology with Clyde. The only worthwhile addition is a character with the wonderful name of Clide Mumpower, but he doesn't seem to do much.

However, there is one exciting development. In place of the portrait of Shepherd which adorned the first edition, there is a picture of a spray of rhododendron. Some see this as merely a picture of a flower, but to those who know, it is obviously a coded reference to Lidie's bosom.

Bibliography

The Balsam Groves of the Grandfather Mountain: a Tale of the Western North Carolina Mountains. Together with Information Relating to the Height of Important Mountains, etc., Banner Elk, 1892; Second edition, 1895; Third 'Rhododendron' edition, 1907

☞ **Four Stars and Better**
Margaret Cavendish; James McIntyre; Joseph Gwyer; Julia Moore; William MacGonagall; Francis Saltus Saltus; Théophile Marzials; Pedro Carolino; Walter Reynolds; Amanda McKittrick Ros

☞ **Tales of Travel**
Bloodgood H. Cutter; Thomas Costley; Pedro Carolino; Frederick James Johnston-Smith

The Five Golden Rules of Bad Writing
4. Memorable . . . For All The Wrong Reasons

Truly bad writing sticks in the memory. Like a splinter in the finger, or a speck of dirt in the eye, it is irritatingly persistent. It is a sad fact of art that the truly bad is so much more memorable than the really good. Not many of us can hum Elgar's Cello Concerto, but we can easily whistle 'The Birdie Song'.

Thus, much as we would like to be able to memorise huge chunks of Shakespeare, Keats and Milton, their glorious words are frequently shoved out of our brain by the genius of those at the opposite end of the spectrum.

For example...
We have already encountered Margaret Cavendish's wonderful line, 'Life scums the cream of Beauty with Time's spoon' and Grainger's 'Now muse, let's sing of rats!' but here are a few more gems:

The opening line of Edward Edwin Foot's poem 'Thought' runs:

> *O silent tickler of the human brain!*

while one of my favourite lines is quoted by J.C. Squire, although he does not know the source:

> *The beetle booms adown the glooms and bumps among the clumps.*

Meanwhile, I will always remember Walter Reynolds's marvellous line from *Young England*, where the scoutmistress says,

> *I must go and attend to my girls' water.*

Like all great art, these lines endure. They have staying power. After all, perfume may be sweet, but, as James Grainger would confirm, manure smells stronger.

Modern Times

Thomas Costley (fl. 1894–5)
The Laureate of Southport

Rome, Paris, Athens, London - just a few of the fabled cities that have inspired poets for centuries. For Thomas Costley, however, none of these held a candle to what was, in his eyes, the most magical and romantic town of them all: Southport.

Sketches of Southport and Other Poems, by Thomas Costley, was published in 1899. As he wrote in the preface:

> *Southport is a most delightful place. I have been to no watering place that has pleased me more for the last thirty-four years to get my annual wash…*

By annual wash, the author means (I hope) bathing in the sea. If he doesn't then I imagine the citizens of Southport viewed his arrival with rather less enthusiasm – especially if the wind was behind him. His wonderful poem 'The Botanic Gardens, Churchtown' puts Southport firmly on a pedestal as the most beautiful town in the world:

> *Southport, once desolate and void of fame,*
> *Has now no peer,[1] if all the beauty it contains*
> *Is set forth truly in descriptive phrase.*
> *Its streets are mudless after copious rains,*
> *And dry before the clouds have passed away.*
> *Each house is free from grime, and weather-stains…*

Indeed, if it has a downside, it is that the unwary visitor might be drunk with too much pleasure. In the following

---

[1] Some experts argue that this is a spelling mistake and what he should have said was, 'Southport has now no pier'.

lines I think he is talking about the exhibits, rather than the museum staff, but he doesn't make it clear.

> *And when the stranger is intoxicate*
> *With too much pleasure, let him turn aside*
> *To view the curious things that have no life,*
> *In the museum…*

To the besotted eye of Thomas Costley, Southport has an almost classical grace to it:

> *Each season she appears more gay,*
> *This best of bathing places;*
> *Like Venus rising from the sea,*
> *Attended by the Graces.*
>
> from 'Southport Shore'

Indeed, his enthusiasm for the town leads him to make some rather extravagant claims. I mean, never mind Waterloo, Trafalgar or Rorke's Drift – if you want glory, Southport is the place:

> *Southport! thy name though not of ancient date,*
> *Nor chosen to delight fastidious ears,*
> *Is dearer than the names that kings have given*
> *To palaces and fields of victory…*
>
> from 'Flora of Southport'

It has to be admitted that the glories described in these poems do not match readily with the idea of Southport as a small English seaside town, and sometimes one has to make a large leap of the imagination to see all that Costley saw. Sometimes, indeed, the real location of these magical landscapes comes as a bit of an anti-climax:

> *Here flowers of all lands and climes are seen,*
> *And lawns kings might tread on or e'en a queen –*
> *Where ceaseless sings the joyful lark*
> *Until the white moon dons her robes of gold –*
> *Wouldst thou enjoy these pleasures manifold?*
> *Then turn thy steps to Hesketh Park.*
>
> from 'Hesketh Park'

It is clear that he valued Southport for more than its classical beauty, its manifold pleasures and the strange, dead things in the museum. It is also a place where he found sympathetic minds – minds given to deep scientific discussion and debate:

> *Dear Friend! I feel constrained in ninety two,*
> *To satisfy a love, no longer new,*
> *That's often drawn my heart to Southport's shore,*
> *And to your flower-environed cottage more.*
> *…*
> *And what was that which drew our souls together*
> *Out of the fickle world's inconstant weather?*
> *'Twas Nature's self: your book of dried fern-leaves*
> *Gave proof of love for her who ne'er deceives.*
> from 'To W.H.S.'

Yes, Southport has it all: beaches, white moons, royal lawns, things that have no life and fascinating collections of dried fern-leaves.

As with many of our bad poets, the preface to his book of verse is littered with commendations from friends and critics:

> *A most talented philosopher and friend, now deceased, writes: – 'Your*
> *"Winter" and "Under the Sycamore Trees" reached me at Southport,*
> *and charmed me. My friends too were much delighted. A live coal*
> *from the sphere of home and rendezvous of Mirth has touched your*
> *lips…'*

There are several problems with this comment, not least the question of how his friend 'writes' if he is deceased. And where, exactly, is 'the sphere of home and rendezvous of Mirth'? Possibly he means nearby Blackpool.

While devoted to Southport, he also wrote on other topics. His poem 'Sir Walter Raleigh' is both informative and stirring:

In Devon, on a village farm, at Hay,
Sir Walter first beheld the light of day;
The month was June, in fifteen fifty-two,
When Edward Tudor reigned, the young and true.
...
When he was sixteen he went to Oriel college,
In search of influence, and a wider knowledge;
In fifteen eighty-four, across the main
Through many a storm, he sailed new lands to gain...

He is also aware of the modern impact of Sir Walter's most famous discovery, helpfully pointing out that very few people wanted tobacco before it had been discovered:

There he discovered what supplies a want
Then felt but little – the tobacco plant –
By moralists denounced, by smokers praised;
The plant from which large revenue is raised.

In 'The Bards of Erin', he also reflects on his Irish ancestry and heritage:

The old Bards of Erin[2] to nature were true
No matter the theme that was under review;
Or whether of king, or of soldier, or river
They sang, the world it must listen for ever.

But perhaps his most ambitious poem is the charmingly titled 'A Metrical Record Of The Autumnal Meeting Of The Congregational Union Of England And Wales, Held At Bradford, October 1892'. This, to be fair, fails to capture fully the passion and excitement of the event, although he makes a brave stab.

Along with congregational matters and, of course, Southport, the other major love of Costley's life was botany. It was something that moved him to raptures of wonder. Take, for instance, his exciting periwinkle:

---

[2] Ireland. In the world of bad poetry, Ireland is always Erin, just as the sun is 'Sol' and the planets 'orbs'. These things have to be done properly, you know.

> *In my little garden, not far from my gate,*
> *A plant is in flower, tho' its blooming is late,*
> *That wondering looks on at the flocks who pass by,*
> *And hears with a blush my praise when I cry,*
> *Hurrah for the peerless periwinkle!*
> from 'The Periwinkle'

One can understand the passing flocks' surprise – it is not every day you pass a front garden and hear someone yelling about his late-blooming periwinkles. But Thomas was prone to shouting out. The same feeling invades his only other book, *My Favourite Authors*, which is probably the only work of literary criticism to include a chapter on botany. Evidently, Costley was running out of material by the end of the book, so he slipped in a chapter on 'The Natural System of Botanical Classification'. In this, he has a similar experience to the periwinkle episode, but this time centred on wallflowers:

> *When it first dawned on me that the wall-flower belonged to the same order as the cabbage; and the Tomato to the same order as the Potato, I exclaimed, 'How wonderful are the works of nature, that combine things so dissimilar, and yet in the most essential part of their organisms so much alike!'*

Sentiments, I think, that we can all share. But despite the exciting botany chapter, *My Favourite Authors* is not Costley at his best. No, for that we have to return to Southport – cosmopolitan metropolis, refined resort and a magnet for cultured people everywhere.

> *I love it as a town … I like it for its free, well-stocked library; for its extensive, and indeed immeasurable, untrodden tracks of sand; for its large and beautiful marine lake; for its esplanades and promenades; and I hope and trust that my sketches of Southport town, in verse, will make it better known so that it may have a greater history in the future than it has had in the past.*

Alas, these days they all go to Disneyland.

Bibliography

Sketches of Southport and Other Poems, Manchester, c. 1895
My Favourite Authors, London, 1894

☞ Tales of Travel
Bloodgood H. Cutter; J.B. Smiley; Pedro Carolino; Shepherd M. Dugger; Frederick James Johnston-Smith

***

Leopold John Manners De Michele (fl. 1896)

Unfulfilled Genius and Pony Patter

Leopold John Manners de Michele is a lost poet. He published only one volume of verse, *Stray Lyrics*, in 1869. After this, it appears that he put away his quill and resigned himself to a career as a solicitor, which is a kind of living death.

His departure from the field was a sad loss to bad poetry, for his slim volume is a wonderful collection of truly awful verse. Much of it is concerned with Leopold's love for a certain woman, whom he can only love from afar. This non-affair is celebrated in the moving love story, 'To B.M.':

> *I saw her and loved her together!*
>   *She stood by the side of the road:*
> *'Twas all 'mid the blossoming heather;*
>   *'Twas close to her charming abode.*
>
> *She came to the side of my chaise:*
>   *We laughed and we merrily chatted;*
> *(And this to her infinite praise,)*
>   *My pony she tenderly patted.*

Expert opinion is divided on the last line. There are some who think that B.M. is a free spirit, an unfettered expression of new womanhood. Others, however, argue that she has gone too far and that you should never pat a gentleman's pony on a first date. Nevertheless, she did, and this one pat is enough to send Leopold's mind reeling:

> *I wished I had been in the shafts!*
>   *One chance of her gentle caress:*
> *True, with harness, for clothing, the draughts*
>   *Would never have suited the dress.*

It is not clear what his meaning is here. He appears to be wishing to change places with the horse, whilst worrying about the suitability of his clothing. There are worrying overtones of Swinburne, but alas all ends in failure:

> I saw her this once, and was undone;[1]
>> And then we met once in the train: –
> She travelled, with maid, up to London;
>> And then – I ne'er saw her again.
>
> But this I shall never forget –
>> The horrible state we were in,
> When once she was soaked with the wet,
>> While I was quite drenched to the skin.

The 'undone'/'London' rhyme is daring. And the final verse is mysterious. With what is she soaked? We know it is wet, but what is it? And is it the same substance that has drenched young Leopold?

It is clear the affair, moist or otherwise, never left Leopold. In the poem 'To The Same'[2] he reveals that his love has fled to sunnier climes:

> They tell me you fly to a scene
>> That is sunny, and glaring, and so on;
> As a swallow goes off with the green,
>> And – I am unable to go on!

Again there is an adjective but no noun. The swallow goes off with the green something but we don't know what. Perhaps it was the same as the wet. Perhaps the wet is not only wet, but green. Perhaps not.

Anyway, he is distraught. But he soon picks himself up, for in another poem, 'To G. From a Distance', he has met another girl. I have never seen any laughing teeth, but I imagine the sight is enough to drive anyone slightly over the edge:

---

[1] I know what you're thinking, and you really ought to know better.
[2] i.e. 'B.M.' again.

Cupids and devils both conspired
*   To bow me down before your grace.*
Minutes that were dreamy – hazy –
*   Laughing teeth, and eyes all fired –*
Thoughts that hovered o'er thy face –
*   Drove me thinking – drove me crazy.*

After his doomed passion for 'B.M,' the reader might be for-
given for thinking that the rest of his poetry would mourn
his lost love. But no. Leopold is made of sterner stuff and we
soon find him flinging himself madly at the first set of laughing teeth that comes along. This may shock the reader, but
let's face it, once you have had your pony patted, you are
bound to take a more relaxed view of human relationships. A
few poems later he is flirting with May:

My pretty May,
*   Whose eyes are bright –*
Whose silken hair is brown to-day –
*   My love requite!*

I long to kiss
*   Those rosy cheeks!*
And after I'd accomplished this,
*   To kiss away for weeks!*

But cast away
*   Those satire sounds*
That clog the flow of what you say,
*   Like coffee grounds!*
The season the most air is that of London –

Where ladies seek the matrimonial noose.
*   I much enjoy to eat, with waistcoat undone,*
The season that exists within the goose.
from 'To May'

The 'London/undone' rhyme is perhaps getting a little stale
by now.

Meanwhile, 'The Unexpected Pleasure' tells of an assignation that went terribly wrong:

> So I crept with my feet, with a thought of retreat –
>> Though whisp'ring, 'my love,' and 'my darling,' and 'dove; –'
> Till, hearing a grin, I was drenched to the skin,
>> From a large pail of water that came from above!!

Again there are several startling phrases in this simple verse. The poet creeps 'with his feet'. Is he carrying them? Or are they moving silently, alongside him? And how, precisely, do you 'hear' a grin? Or is he, perhaps, indicating that the lady's teeth were laughing again?

The volume, I am happy to say, is not entirely taken up with love songs. 'Immatra' tells of his voyage to Finland and begins

> Hail! Finland's solitary haunts!
> Oh, wild and pointed scenery...

And he brings the roughness of the sea to dramatic life:

> Look down, traveller, and quake!
>> Hast thou been upon the main,
> When the good ships timbers shake,
>> And your whiskers drip with rain

He seems to spend a lot of time in wet conditions; he is the wettest poet I know.

Much of his poetry is drawn from the gritty realities of life. In his poem 'On Contemplating the Mechanics Paper, 1866' he faces up to the dreadful possibility of failure:

> Shuddering – with pallid face –
>> I went through the worst of panics,
> As I made a foul grimace
>> At the paper in mechanics.

> Silver's gravity is ten:
>> Twenty-one is that of platinum.
> I did not think that there was then
>> So great a difference as that in 'em.

And in 'Election Poem' he brings his biting satire to work on the vagaries of government:

> *Oh Pedlington! the chosen of the mob!*
> *'Twere better had you nestled in the war*
> *Of commerce, than have lived to sob,*
> *Rejected, as your better h's are.*
>
> *For scarce a month had yet elapsed*
> *Ere sanguinest electors forced their smiles, –*
> *And looking at each other, hoped, – perhapsed, –*
> *And went to catch fresh voters with their wiles:*
>
> *But all in vain: the struggle soon arrived, –*
> *And coalition triumphed as of yore;*
> *And foes of Pedlington somehow contrived*
> *For every vote of his to show him two or more.*

Again there are many fine features here, such as the phrase 'your better h's', which presumably means 'your better halves' (but still makes no sense), and the wonderful invented word 'perhapsed' – a stroke of genius which was obviously the result of a desperate search for a rhyme for 'elapsed'.

I do not know what happened to Leopold after he entered the law. It is one of the tragedies of literature that he never again published any verse. Maybe someone knows what he went on to do. Maybe, hidden away in a dusty old solicitor's office, is a small collection of poems full of laughing teeth and people getting wet.

Or perhaps he turned his undoubted skills to his chosen profession. Perhaps we should remember him as he undoubtedly must have been, leaning insouciantly against the dock, persuading the judge of some important point with his flowing eloquence, whilst at the same time eyeing up a female member of the jury and hoping that someday she might be persuaded to pat his pony.

Bibliography

Stray Lyrics, Oatlands Park, Surrey, 1869

☞ Made-Up Words and Strange Syntax
'Lord' Timothy Dexter; Théophile Marzials; Pedro Carolino; Nancy Luce; Amanda McKittrick Ros

☞ Minor Victorians
Eliza Cook; Stephen Fawcett; J. Stanyan Bigg; Alfred Austin; Pownoll Toker Williams

✱✱✱

J. Gordon Coogler (1865–1901)
Poems while you wait

Coogler had a print shop in Charleston, South Carolina, with a sign outside saying 'Poems Written While You Wait'. Personally, I am surprised that his poems took that long, many of them giving the impression of having been knocked off whilst the customer was still entering the shop.

They were collected in successive editions of his seminal work, *Purely Original Verse* – a book which sold thousands of copies in his lifetime, albeit for the wrong reasons. There were even Coogler fan clubs.[1] Perhaps his most famous lines are contained in the following immortal couplet, lamenting the dearth of writers in the southern States:

> *Alas for the South, her books have grown fewer,*
> *She never was much given to literature.*

Born in 1865 in Blythwood, South Carolina, he is pictured in the front of his book, a young, serious man with a huge waxed moustache. Indeed, facial hair, or rather the lack of it, features more than once in his poetry, particularly in his poem, 'A Mustachless Bard':

> *His whiskers didn't come, his mustache is gone*
> *And today he's standing ashore*
> *Enjoying the breeze, with a cleaned shaved lip*
> *Relieved of the burden it bore.*

---

[1] The Atlanta fan club acknowledged a picture of Coogler with the words 'Each and every member wanted to take the picture from the packing with his own hands...'

> *He's feeling so lonely, dull and foresaken,*
> *The boys they know him no more;*
> *The girls are surprised, and speaking of him*
> *Say, 'He's uglier than ever before.'*

A warning to us all: don't shave your face, you are probably uglier than you think.

His poetry also contains much cautionary advice for women. 'More Care for the Neck than the Intellect' is a dire warning to all young women who care more for their bosoms than their brains.

> *Fair lady on that snowy neck and half-clad bosom*
> *Which you so publicly reveal to man,*
>   *There's not a single stain or speck;*
> *Would you had given but half the care*
> *To the training of your intellect and heart*
>   *As you have given to that spotless neck.*

He goes on to meditate on the fate of the lady's chest:

> *For Time, alas! must touch with cold unnerring hand,*
> *That fair bosom's soft, untarnished hue...*

As all ladies will testify, there is nothing worse than a cold unerring hand on your bosom. But Coogler, it has to be said, had an ambivalent attitude towards bosoms. Sometimes he condemns them, at other times he wants nothing more than to go to sleep on them:

> *How sweet when our lonely soul grows weary*
>   *And our tired feet need rest,*
> *To recline 'neath the shade of the willow tree,*
>   *Pillow's on a maiden's breast.*

> *To feel a passion pure within us,*
>   *And not the one that seeks to rob*
> *That beautiful virtue underlying*
>   *Her peaceful bosom's throb.*

Whilst another popular fashion of the day is attacked in 'Pull Of [sic] Those Suspenders':

> Sweet girl I like to see you look
> The very best you can
> But please do not try so soon
> To imitate a man.
>
> You are not masculine or neuter,
> Neither of those genders;
> Therefore I'd advise you to
> Take off those suspenders.[2]

Coogler was a Methodist Sunday School teacher, a background which can be clearly seen in the following lines:

> The man who thinks God is too kind
> To punish actions vile,
> Is bad at heart, of unsound mind
> Or very juvenile.

There is, indeed, a certain streak of the judgemental about his work:

> She was beautiful once: but she fell,
>   And some said 'let her go,'
> For she can never shine again
>   Like a beautiful flake of snow.

But ultimately he spends more time celebrating women than condemning them:

> On her beautiful face there are smiles of grace
>   That linger in beauty serene,
> And there are no pimples encircling her dimples,
>   As ever, as yet, I have seen.

---

[2] 'Suspenders' in this context means, of course what the British call braces. At least I hope it means braces. If not, it puts a very different slant on this poem.

Coogler died tragically young. 'My style and my sentiments are MY OWN,' he wrote, 'purely original.' The *Charleston News and Courier* said that he was an excellent young man, who 'unfortunately thought he was a poet'.

But perhaps the last word should go to the critic Charles A. Dana, who in a careful choice of words, summed Coogler up.

> *He writes verse as no other man has ever written. The country owes much to J. Gordon Coogler.*

And what is more, his clients didn't even have to wait long.

Bibliography

Purely Original Verse with Original Reviews and a Biographical Sketch, 1897 (Photographical reprint, Columbia, 1974)

☞ Bosom Fanatics

George Wither; J. Gordon Coogler; Francis Saltus Saltus; Théophile Marzials

***

William Nathan Stedman (fl. 1900—1916)
Bookseller, Publisher, Poetic Stalker

Apart from believing that William Gladstone was the Antichrist, and ruled the world through hypnotic powers, William Nathan Stedman was as sane as the next man.

Admittedly he also believed that he was destined to marry the Victorian novelist Marie Corelli, but anyone can get a bit obsessed about their favourite author. And I am certain that when he said that he had been offered the Poet Laureateship, together with £30,000 and the Prime Minister's daughter thrown in, he was telling nothing but the truth. Probably.

Oh, all right, William Nathan Stedman is one of the more eccentric of the world's worst writers, which, considering the company, is going some. He was born at Brighton in 1861 and lived for most of his life in Watford and north London, apart from a short spell in Australia. He was a poet, theologian, philosopher, playwright and borderline madman.

His earliest work – and I think his best (or at least his funniest, which amounts to the same thing) – is his verse drama *The Man in the Moon*, written in 1907. It is mercifully free from the paranoia and Gladstone-bashing that features so heavily in his later writings. Self published from the premises of his stationer's business in Watford, it is a sprightly *jeu d'esprit*, mixing fantasy, science fiction and social realism together with some Norse gods in disguise and some entertainingly bad writing. The play is subtitled

A MUSICAL MERRY-GO-ROUND and SATIRICAL ALLEGORY, wherein the FOOL may see himself; the WISE may learn and laugh; and think: and ALL may find reason, wit, humour and truth; and a round of genuine amusement.

BY
Wm NATHAN STEDMAN
Loet Paureat
Aye, come with me, and I will show you many things, as in a Glass,
freed from the silly skirts of mock-modesty.

I can't wait. My mock-modest skirts have been feeling tight of late. The work, printed in red and green ink, begins with a comment from the author:

> *Many authors write prefaces, generally a sign of puerile weakness, praying for critical mercy and all manner of hotch-potch. We do nothing of the sort for ourselves, being conscious of a prime knowledge of the world, its falsities, its frailties, general frothiness and red mantled fornications.*

Having said that he wouldn't write a preface, he then goes on to write one, full of his trademark invective and self-belief:

> *we deplore and despise the petty pretences of persons who live on make-believe and rotten vanity. That is why, in our Light-Winged chariot yclept 'Dramatic Poetry', we carry the sword of Truth in one hand, and the whip of Satire in the other.*

If he's carrying a sword in one hand and a whip in the other I don't know who's steering the thing. But then again, Stedman does give the impression of a man out of control. Most of all, he seems to have it in for a type of person he describes as 'the Gilt-brained Pup', whose 'proper portion is a pauper lunatic asylum here and hell hereafter', whose 'insanity is a hereditary birthright' and at whom the 'Scions of Wisdom in the Infinite Realms of eternity, look down in disgust and derision also at the vicious cad who poses as The Gilt Brained PUP.'

The dramatis personae of this remarkable work includes such characters as Mr Compos Mentis (The Man in the Moon in mufti), Proffessor [sic] Rainbow (A savant, who builds an astral ship), Lord Fitzfoodle, and Sandy MacGregor (Scotch shepherd who owns a set of bagpipes and sixpence). The female characters include several fairies, also in mufti, the goddess Venus and Miss Fanny Folly, a fast young woman.

Adventurously, the dialogue is entirely in rhyme, which gives the whole work the feel of a pantomime:

> PROFESSOR: *The dinners here are good,*
>   *That's generally understood.*
>   *I cannot answer for the comp'ny though.*
>   *But those who pay the price*
>   *Need not be over-nice.*
>   *The club is Cosmopolitan, you know.*
> COMPOS MENTIS: *So here we meet with friends.*
>   *What happiness depends*
>   *Upon a wise and good gastronomy.*
> PROFESSOR: *I suppose,*
>   *On that builds all he knows*
>   *within his mind of vast astronomy.*

There is another character, called William Wilder, who is infatuated with 'Mornaneve Venus', particularly her knees, resulting in one of Stedman's best rhymes:

> WILDER: *Your limb is a beauty!*
>   *A vision your knee!*
> VENUS: *Fie, fie, sir, don't tarry, –*
>   *'Honi soit qui mal y –'*
>   *For by the lord Harry*
>   *I'm on strict modesty.'*

Scene 2 has a more urban feel as we are introduced to PC Cuff Collar and the nine-year-old loveable scamp, 'Boy Mischief':

> *(Enter Boy Mischief.)*

> BOY: *Please sir, I've lost my way*
>   *And should thank you to say*
>   *If Cockspur Street's at hand.*
>   *They say it's near the Strand.*

PC: *Down there.*
BOY: *Down where?*
PC: *Down THERE.*
BOY: *A well-known thoroughfare*
  Where cock fights used to be.
  Cock fights with SPURS, you see.
PC: *Oh!*
BOY: *So.*
PC: *Ah!*
BOY: *Yah!*
PC: *Cock spurs?*
BOY: *Yes. Steel spurs called 'COCKSPURS'.'*

After this deathless piece of dialogue, the boy runs off and the PC sings

> *When I am off duty*
> *My cookie's a beauty*
> *Behind the kitchen door.*
> *Beer and beef and mutton*
> *Suits me to a button,*
> *I put away a store.*
> *I tickle her with my staff*
> *And I make the cookie laugh –*

We are then introduced to Giles, a country bumpkin, O'Flyn, an Irish labourer, and MacGregor, who enters playing his bagpipes.

The play is liberally sprinkled with songs, which remind one inescapably of Belgian entries to the Eurovision Song Contest:

> *Ring, ingle, dang, dong,*
> *My hard iron song*
> *In the old belfry sung.*
> *Dong, dangle, ring, ding,*
> *With flustering wing*
> *Sped by each iron tongue.*
> *All through the bleak air*

My messengers fair –
White snowflakes are tumbled and tossed
To tell that I'm coming, King frost.
Ring, ding, ding, ring, ring, ding, dang, dong.
Ring, ding, dang, dong.
Ding, dang, dong.
Dang, dong.
D-O-N-G.[1]

In Act Two, Fairies Sunshine and Twilight appear and, in a radical departure, talk about the play in prose, discussing the vices of the rich and the need for better sanitation, along the way having another shot at 'the gilt-brained pups' who send 'vast batches of game… To various institutions of so-called charity'.

In the final scene the various travellers congregate to fly off in the Professor's spaceship. A series of wonderful transformations take place, in which Mrs Night throws off her 'widow's garments' revealing herself to be 'a beautiful fairy, enrobed in silver and star-spangled vestments', Compos, the Professor and others appear in Greek togas, and the author has another go at the GBPs:

> *The gilt-brained pups are to be most heartily congratulated on their future rewards, the dung-heaps of death and damnation.*

Perhaps the most astonishing transformation is that of William Wilder, who throws off his motor garb to appear as a Scandinavian Sea King. He sings a song which mysteriously mentions 'gases':

> *I sweep all the lands in my flight,*
> *Grasping all gases galore,*
> *Which arise by day and by night,*
> *Dropping them far from each shore.*

---

[1] See also 'The Sun of my Songs' by Théophile Marzials, another poet who enjoyed donging.

My chemical action is wise
  Ordained for the good of the world.
Far from the haunts of men I arise.
  Resting, my pinions are furled.

The hatch is closed, and propelled by William's gases they fly off to a better world.

In *The Man In The Moon* other dramatic works by William Nathan Stedman are listed, including *The Duke's Daughter*, *King James The First* and *The Uncrowned Queen*. However, the only one I have been able to find is *King Edward the Seventh*, which is included as an appendix to a book catalogue he issued in 1913.[2]

This is a very different work from *The Man in the Moon*. It is set in the court of Edward VII and Queen Alexandra, but written in a strange, quasi-Shakespearian blank verse.

The king, for example, begins a council by saying:

My princes, peers and noble councillors,
It is our royal will that Ireland
Be visited by us th'ensuing week
In hopes that peace will spread prosperity.

And, when warned about the possibility of attack, he cries:

Gog's Wouns! gallant Murray, Scotch caution is yours:
An attribute suited to generals in war.

It is somehow hard to reconcile this manner of speaking with the real figure of Edward VII, who was more of a hunting, shooting, fishing, sleeping-with-numerous-royal-mistresses kind of chap.

The play is a short work which tells of a plot to assassinate the King. The conspirators are foiled by one Jack Hornpipe, a sailor, who captures the plotters before tearing off his disguise:

(Jack tears off his disguise and hands back the gun.)

---

[2] Which includes an advert for *The Man in the Moon*, bound in morocco, price 3/6d. A bargain if ever I saw one.

> *I know both King and Queen will do their best*
> *To comfort Ireland and redress her wrongs.*
> *Ye are at fault to hatch foul murder here,*
> *To scheme 'gainst him who never did ye harm,*
> *To seek curst means to break the laws of God,*
> *And bring damnation on your own sad souls.*
> *See here, now look, I doff this uniform,*
> *Tear off this beard and wig, the whole disguise, –*
> *Give back to you this weapon holding death*
> *And stand before you thus a 'fenceless man.*
> *Ye know my face. And now the truth shall ring*
> *On opened ears and hearts and everything,*
> *That can to you a swift conviction bring, –*
> *For I am he – now shoot – I AM THE KING!*

Yes, it was Edward VII all along. Naturally, the conspirators are all overwhelmed by this heroic act and immediately fall at his feet in repentance.

In the afterword to this play, Stedman is justly proud of the significance of the work:

> *That a good national poem does make its mark, I have ample evidence for knowing. I have met ladies and gentlemen, years after its publication, in India, in the South Sea Islands, in Italy, in South America, in France, in Spain, in Egypt and in the Australian states who have treasured copies of this comedy and expressed their admiration of it.*

He goes on to say that

> *As a poet born and bred it is my office and privilege to point out things which escape general attention…*

A statement that many feel sums up Stedman's life and art. The facts which have escaped most general attention, but which to Stedman are as clear as day, are the genius of Marie Corelli and the evil of Gladstone. In his book *Sonnets Lays And Lyrics*, he claims that he was, in fact, offered the Poet Laureateship, but turned it down:

> *The beautiful gift of poetic genius was ever intended for the service of God and not for prostitution to mammon, not for the antics of a court-paid, wee-piping buffoon; (an office which I refused after Tennyson's death, though made with the offer of the premier's daughter and £30,000.)*

Curiously there is no historical record of this offer.

His sonnets are unusual in that they all consist of nine lines, in defiance of the usual conventions. They are mostly humdrum affairs, although I did enjoy Sonnet 68 which begins:

> *The big-bellied globe draws near to the hour*
> *When it must deliver to HIS high power...*

and the tribute to God's adding up in Sonnet 77:

> *I tell you that He never makes mistakes.*
> *His algebra correct is for our sakes.*

The book is illustrated with a bizarre collection of engravings from an old copy of *The Pilgrim's Progress*, all except Sonnet 84 which is illustrated with a Louis Wain print of some cats.

In *Lays and Lyrics* his devotion to Mrs Corelli comes to the fore. Perhaps the heat of Australia (where this was published) was firing his passions.The book starts rather aggressively, addressed to

> *'Queen Marie, My lance against the world for its Greatest Lady. Any Man, Beast or Buffoon want SMASHING?'*

Stedman appears to have declared himself her unofficial husband:

> *None of you, YOU ye scrofulous swine-hounds, could compose a page of Any of the books written by your Queen ... 'Tis not a woman speaking to you now, but HER HUSBAND, who CAN and WILL slog, slosh and SCRAGG the whole damned pack of ye, IN ONCE.*

Lest we take him lightly, he obviously has the muscle to back up his threats:

if any future attack is intended upon THIS LADY, and the writer or speaker will muster sufficient temerity to send me his name and abode, one of my 7ft Zulus (faithful fellows) will promptly attend – distance and expense immaterial – with his sjambok and FULL INSTRUCTIONS WHAT TO DO.

There is something awe-inspiring about the picture of one of Stedman's seven-foot Zulus turning up on your doorstep with a loaded sjambok and a full set of instructions. Although the phrase 'distance and expense immaterial' is unfortunate – it sounds as if Stedman is going to pop his Zulu in the post.

The poems once again fail to live up to the promise of the foreword, although there is a nice sense of yearning to the poem 'The Lord is Mindful of his Own', where Marie finally realizes that William is the man for her.

Marie plays the harp and the music forms a 'Sqirit [sic] shape':

> *And then she raised her voice*
> *In accents full of life;*
> *She sang in strains truth*
> *'Ah yes, I'll be his wife.'*
> *Spirit Echo – 'Ah, yes, you'll be his wife.*
> *Be his wife.*
> *His w-i-f-e.'*

This does not make for comfortable reading. It is the poetic equivalent of stalking. However, while this obsession with Marie Corelli might be considered mildly eccentric, his theories about Gladstone are positively weird. They are revealed in full in his fascinating theological treatise, *Antichrist and the Man of Sin*, modestly subtitled

> *THE MOST IMPORTANT WORK IN MODERN HISTORY*
> *SPECIAL TO EVERY INDIVIDUAL ON EARTH*

His preface gives the impression of a man of common sense:

Faithless minded men, ever seeking to learn yet neve [sic] learning think, speak, write and publish all sorts of theories, tomfooleries more or less insane, (generally more) and sciences falsely called. And some most extraordinary notions have been foisted on the world. They have no place...

After which he goes on to develop one of the weirdest theories ever put into print. The nub of his theory is dramatically revealed in a piece of numerology:

And here is The Man's Name and the Correct Counting of his Number in the Greek of Saint John's Book of Divine Revelations; –

Name	Number
Gamma	*3*
Lambda	*30*
Alpha	*1*
Delta	*4*
Sigma	*200*
Tau	*300*
Omicron	*70*
Nu	*50*
Eta	*8*
GLADSTONE	*666*

He unhelpfully refuses to explain the basis of these numbers, choosing merely to say:

Understand? All clear. All reasonable. All righteous.

Gladstone is therefore revealed as the Antichrist – a fact which must have come as a shock to Mrs Gladstone. Stedman himself has seen the beast in his lair:

Let those living now who saw (as I have myself) his Great Black Eyes glinting with Satan's fierce and sombre haze, in the House of Commons... Going on in this terrible career, he elevated himself in secret, keeping the possession of his Black Art close to himself, and no man knew that he was a great and powerful mesmerist, who could see and hear all round the world...

What's more, Gladstone was not just limiting his heinous crimes to the House of Commons, he was getting out a bit as well:

> *Any faithful man who is at all familiar with Physiognomy, has only to look at any of the photographs of Gladstone during the years 1887 1888 and 1889 to see the real author of the shocking Whitechapel Mysteries, murders by deputy, both victims and medium – 'Jack the Ripper' – being under the infernal mesmerism of Gladstone: perpetrated 'in the divine fury of his wrath' for being ousted out of parliament over the Irish question of Home Rule.*

This is a new twist on the Jack the Ripper murders. As far as I can recall, no one has ever proposed the theory that they were committed by a sitting Prime Minister in response to an unsuccessful vote in Parliament.

Chapter eight starts with a description of Gladstone's appearance:

> *But the image of God in him vanished in after years. He more resembled a wild beast. The world was astonished to learn that HIS HEAD GREW LARGER … He shows the Head of the Greatest Unhung Criminal.*

His head grew larger? Surely someone would have noticed. Surely the Queen, in one of her regular consultations with the Prime Minister, would have enquired about his expanding hat size?

Stedman was obviously gloriously talented and more than a little unhinged. He was never strictly insane – although he did live in East Finchley, which is hardly the sign of a balanced mind. For most of his life he ran a bookshop, and I can't imagine that his customers saw him as anything other than mildly eccentric.

The press comments printed in his books give the impression of a sane and reasonable man. 'Our brilliant townsman', said the *Brighton Gazette*, and 'Noble thoughts in melodious language', claimed the *Elocutionist*. Queen Alexandra is quoted as saying 'Fragrant and beautiful', although whether she is talking about William or his poems is not made clear. Significantly, the Marquis of Salisbury describes him as 'A genius, a gentleman and a hero'. But then Salisbury was a Conservative and Gladstone was a Liberal. So you'd expect him to say that, really.

Maybe, however, there were occasional glimpses. Maybe, every now and then, a customer would ask for something by Marie Corelli only to see a seraphic smile pass across his face. Or maybe, on the other hand, an unwary customer would enter the shop and ask for the Life of Gladstone, only to find himself thrown out of the door, pursued by a hail of invective and a hurled copy of *The Man in the Moon*, bound in Morocco and priced at 3/6d.

Bibliography

The Man In The Moon – A Musical Merry-go-round And Satirical Allegory, Watford, 1907

Antichrist and The Man of Sin, Watford, 1909

Sonnets Lays and Lyrics, Sydney, 1911

What Might Have Been – Ballads & Poems for Reading and Reciting, Sydney, 1912

Stedman's Book Circular, East Finchley, 1913; includes his drama 'King Edward the Seventh'

Sky Blue Ballads; The 'Finchley Press' Poems, East Finchley, 1916

☞ Philosophy and Theology
Margaret Cavendish; The Devout Salutationist;'Lord' Timothy Dexter; Eliza Cook; Keith Odo Newman

☞ Plays and Verse Drama
James Henry Powell; Francis Saltus Saltus; Walter Reynolds

Hero Worship

Bad Poets on Their Fellow Bards

Like all great artists, our bad poets have drawn inspiration from a variety of sources. Here are just a few of their tributes to artists at the other end of the spectrum.

James McIntyre sums up the life of Shelley in one superb stanza:

> *We have scarcely time to tell thee*
> *Of the strange and gifted Shelly,*
> *Kind hearted man but ill-fated,*
> *So youthful, drowned and cremated.*

Edward Edwin Foot, pays a wonderful tribute to Shakespeare – a playwright who would have done the world of English Literature a great service if he'd used a few footnotes himself. In Edward's poem, the image of God tickling Shakespeare's head to produce a load of sarcasm is fascinating:

> *Will's cloudy days nigh spent, his sun arose!*
> *(God with him, tickling his fair brow and sparkling eye)*
> *With wisdom wrote he'n majesty*
> *On high-born kings and lowly peasantry*
> *In rhyme's sweet readings; lines of quaint sarcastic prose...*

It is a remarkable fact that virtually all bad poets seem to hold Robert Burns in deep reverence. It may be because he was a peasant, writing in simple dialect. Or it may be because he wrote a truly terrible poem about a haggis. Whatever the case, he is viewed with awe by many of our writers. Whilst in Scotland, Bloodgood H. Cutter made the pilgrimage to Burns's birthplace and was immediately struck by the muse:

Although I'm aged and careworn
I came to see where Burns was born;
And when I gazed upon the bed
Poetic thoughts rushed in my head.

Not very poetic thoughts, apparently. Byron was another favourite, inspiring Julia Moore to produce one of the least effective rhymes in history:

He had joined the Grecian Army;
This man of delicate frame;
And there he died in a distant land,
And left on earth his fame.
Lord Byron's age was 36 years,
Then closed the sad career,
Of the most celebrated Englishman
Of the nineteenth century.
from *Sketch of Lord Byron's Life*

While J. Gordon Coogler, seems to blame the 'mad, bad and dangerous' Lord's faults squarely on his mother:

Thou immortal Byron!
Thy inspired genius
    Let no man attempt to smother –
May all that was good within thee
Be attributed to Heaven,
    All that was evil – to thy mother.
from *Byron*

This may, however, be a case of taking hero worship too far. As one reviewer said of this poem,

Byron's mother may not have been an admirable woman ... but she died many years ago and we protest that J. Gordon Coogler has no right to rake up any old scandal about her, especially in an ode to her talented son.

Frederick James Johnston-Smith (fl. 1900–1915)

Weird, Gloomy and Horrible

Frederick Johnston-Smith wrote a great many patriotic songs, celebrating the British Empire and all its dominions. His poem on 'Niagara Falls', however, suffers from a sense of anti-climax. All that way and he can't think of anything to say:

> Hail! – Hail, glorious Niagara! – All hail!
> This pilgrimage long years I've deemed a duty;
> And now, I feel my tongue must sadly fail
> To do full justice to thy wondrous beauty…

But it is his epic poem, 'The Captain of the Dolphin', which provides the most satisfaction from a bad poet point of view. The poem opens in an inn in Cornwall, when enters a stranger:

> Our talk was weird, well suited to the night –
> such talk as stirs the human brain and breast;
> And, while the clock was striking twelve, there came
> A bearded, weird and unexpected guest.

It is not Richard Branson, however, but a sort of Ancient Mariner Junior. He tells the story of how he left his young wife in Dundee and set off, captaining the 'Dolphin' on a voyage of seal-hunting in Canada. It is a strange tale in which the Captain falls into a trance and gets put into a coffin, recovers to save his vessel during a storm and then encounters a phantom ship on the way home:

> Sea-worms had eaten through the sides and through the mouldered deck;
> And we beheld the ghastly ribs of the uprising wreck.
> On plank and rib and rusty bolt the sombre seaweed hung
> And, dragged from out profoundest depths, uncouthest creatures clung.

Like all truly bad writers, he is not above inventing words when necessary.

> *Reluctant I leave, like a lover who goes*
> *From the side of the maid of his choice,*
> *By whom he is held with a cord actuose*
> *Spun out of her beauty and voice.*

It is not entirely clear what 'a cord actuose' is. Presumably it is a nautical term of some kind. It is not explained in the glossary at the back of the poem (although he does tell us, unhelpfully, that 'Derelict' means 'an abandoned ship' and that 'Outward-bound' means 'sailing away from home'). But 'actuose', like all the words he uses which we really need to know about, remains unexplained.

Meanwhile our Ancient Mariner lookalike is sailing into unknown seas, the description of which shows Johnston-Smith at his best. I particularly liked his picture of the arctic winter:

> *Where the sun circles round for the half of the year*
> *And is cold – like a yellow balloon.*

Whilst the sea, far from being threatening, appears to have been cowed into submission:

> *A balminess the darkened hours had brought from out*
>   *the south,*
> *Each breaker doffed its cap of white and shut its*
>   *blatant mouth.*

One can picture the nautical scene: the Captain standing on the poop, tugging on his actuose cord and yelling at the waves, 'Oi! Shut your blatant mouths!'

But such delights are few and far between. The poem is rather long, and inevitably the reader gets a bit lost – not unlike the Captain of the Dolphin. I know that his wife died and then he went to Cornwall, and then there was a wreck which inspired the glorious line:

So deep was she a soggy log she seemed...

But ultimately, I have to admit I gave up. I don't feel I am entirely alone. Press comments about 'The Captain of the Dolphin' ranged from

> *The author's vocabulary and style are somewhat unusual*
> The Athenæum

to

> *The Captain of the Dolphin is weird, gloomy, horrible sometimes...*
> Leeds Mercury

He also wrote a book called *'Flashes from a Lighthouse,'* which is a lot less interesting than it sounds.

Bibliography

The Captain of the Dolphin and Other Poems, London, 1897

☞ Boats and Trains
Thomas Baker; Reverend Edward Dalton; *Titanic* Poets

☞ Tales of Travel
Bloodgood H. Cutter; J.B. Smiley; Thomas Costley; Pedro Carolino; Shepherd M. Dugger

**

The Titanic Poets (1912)
Disasters in Verse

The loss of the *Titanic* in 1912 was one of the greatest disasters in maritime history. Some 1,500 people lost their lives[1] and throughout the world communities were devastated.

Still, it's an ill wind that blows no good, and the disaster did at least produce the delightful volume *Poetical Tributes on the Loss of the Titanic*, which was rushed out in time to capture the public mood.

The book is filled with poems submitted by the public to various newspapers and magazines up and down the country. One man, – Charles F. Forshaw LL.D., decided to collect the best of them, although 'best' here is a relative term. He wrote in his introduction:

> *Great public calamities set the world's heart vibrating in sympathetic accord.*
>
> *But even articulate horror is comparatively transient in its chastening effect, unless fixed on some more retentive medium than the human heart. This is furnished by the records of historian and poet. Without the Iliad, how much should we have known of the fall of Troy?…*

A good point, although some might say that the introduction of Homer at this point raises unfair expectations. Indeed, Mr Forshaw seems to realize this, for he immediately prepares the reader for what is to follow:

> *The reader's indulgence is claimed for any imperfections due to accidents of birth or station. Some of the finest ideas are in many cases*

---

[1] Including Leonardo Di Caprio.

contained in verses of faulty construction, diction or metre, whilst
poems unimpeachable in those respects are often deficient in spirit or
originality.

His warnings are hardly necessary, for the book is full of
absolute gems. The Rev. Robert Atherton, writing in the
Liverpool Daily Mercury, sets the tone with a rather classical
version of events:

> *Gone! Gone! she has gone! And we thought her stupendous!*
> *We called her 'Titanic' to show she was great!*
> *But now there has come a sensation tremendous,*
> *And she has sunk down in the depths to her fate!*
> *...*
> *Gigantic, stupendous, tremendous, 'Titanic!'*
> *The mightiest that rode o'er the acres of foam!*
> *Thy glory, departed, has ended in panic!*
> *The Vandals have sacked an Imperial Rome!*
> *The vandalic icebergs the waters infesting,*
> *Have sunk, as it were, in a moment of time,*
> *The pride of the ocean, the ship that was cresting*
> *The wide-rolling waves with her motion sublime!*

While Francis Thompson, of the *Burton Observer*, starts
almost playfully:

> *Somewhere, away in the Arctic, where the seals and the walrus play,*
> *The Frost-King started his winter's work at the close of an autumn*
> *day...*

He goes on to attribute the sinking to the Frost-King, the
Storm-Fiend and the Ice-King – a theory that, it may be
safely said, has never been fully investigated. William S.
Cormack rather understates, one feels, the impact of the
iceberg:

> *There on the bridge, the Captain*
> *Stood watching the glistening ice,*
> *Whilst fate, unseen by mortal eyes,*
> *Was tossing the deadly dice,*

> *Then two sharp taps on the vessel's side –*
> *And the noise of the engines quickly died.*

Indeed, he treats the whole affair rather matter-of-factly. It is nice to know that everyone kept themselves busy, but I can't help feeling the wireless operator could have made his message a bit snappier:

> *Soon the deck was all alive*
> *With the passengers and crew*
> *And everyone of that vessel*
> *Found plenty of work to do.*
> *And the operator in his room*
> *Tapped out, 'Come quickly, prevent our doom.'*

Agnes Campbell paints a different version of events. In her poem the wireless operator, though heroic, sends an even more cryptic message:

> *And the wireless operator, whose heart was filled with dread,*
> *Sent out the urgent message, 'We are sinking by the head!'*
> *And Philip's hand*
> *By sticking to the wireless, saved seven hundred fellow men.*[2]
> *Such heroism could never be pictured by a pen,*
> *For it was grand.*

And her account of the impact is more mysterious than alarming:

> *'Twas past eleven o'clock at night the stealthy scratching came,*
> *But no-one seemed to realise that scratch their ship would lame,*
> *She was so strong.*
> *But men below were searching, for the damage greater seemed*
> *Than anyone upon that ship had ever thought or dreamed.*
> *The scratch was long.*

---

[2] But not, unfortunately, Leonardo Di Caprio.

Arthur Holmes chose a difficult rhyme scheme, although he solved his difficulty by frequently rhyming the word Titanic with the word, er … Titanic.

> Across a sea
> Of mystery
> A boat of a build Britannic.
> All night, all day,
> Well on her way,
> Wonder of works, mechanic.
>
> Midst dance and song
> They glide along
> The throng, on the gay Titanic.
> They knew no fear,
> For home was here,
> At home, on the gay Titanic.
>
> That night – no light,
> No sail in sight,
> A whisper went round, – no panic;
> A tale was told
> That paled the bold
> She's holed, – is the great Titanic.
>
> Out with the boats!
> Out with the floats!
> Aye out with a will – mechanic!
> The weakest wept,
> Some, still they slept,
> To drown on the doomed Titanic.

I don't know what a 'will – mechanic!' is. And neither, I suspect, did Arthur Holmes.

Robert Hey, writing in the *Whitby Gazette*, is a rhymester of a different sort.[3] His work has a pleasant MacGonagall-esque strain to it.

---

[3] i.e. even worse.

> A fine, noble ship was completed at last,
> For the great White Star Line by a firm at Belfast;
> 'Twas built of material which no doubt was the best,
> And ranked foremost in splendour among all the rest.
>
> …
>
> But when this great ship drew near to mid-ocean,
> The brave captain, no doubt, used every precaution,
> For just about here many icebergs appear,
> And his duty was to steer the ship clear…
> When all of a sudden this splendid ship crashed
> Right into an iceberg they hoped to have passed.

He makes it sound more like a traffic accident. But if Mr Hey's work suffers from being rather mundane, Vincent McNabb from the *Tablet* is positively exotic:

> Ye brothers of the Son whose rood
> Stood up empurpled with a flood
> Or urgent world redeeming blood.

I'd rather not think about it. The book is full of the same recurring imagery – a floating city, leviathan, Babel, the band playing 'Nearer my God to thee', the hubris of man's challenge to nature, the stiff-upper-lipped British stoicism of the passengers and crew.[4]

It is strangely fitting, I suppose, that a tragic maritime disaster should inspire such a tragic poetic disaster. All these writers sailed forth on the sea of poetry – and all of them, without exception, were sunk. I leave the last word to Arthur M. Wingfield, writing so movingly in the *Littlehampton News*:

> A sudden thud! resounding crash!!
> Then, on our minds, burst like a flash
> The awful truth. That fearful sound
> Was caused by the liner as she ground
> Her way into the mighty berg of ice
> That rent her bottom in a trice.

[4] Especially Leonardo Di Caprio.

Bibliography

Poetical Tributes on the Loss of the Titanic, ed. Chas. F.
    Forshaw, LL.D., London, 1912

☞ Death, Disaster and Disease
James Henry Powell; Eliza Cook; Julia Moore; William
MacGonagall; Amanda McKittrick Ros

☞ Boats and Trains
Reverend Edward Dalton; Frederick James Johnston-Smith;
Thomas Baker

****

Walter Reynolds (fl. 1935)
Worst Ever Playwright

Young England, *which celebrated the completion of a six months'*
run by transferring to the Piccadilly Theatre last night, is beginning
to show some of the weaknesses of a dramatic old age. The audience
are definitely over-rehearsed.

In 1967, Mel Brooks made *The Producers*, a film where a
bizarre musical based around the life of Hitler became a success because it was so hilariously awful. What (I presume) he
didn't know is that over thirty years earlier a similar event
happened for real on the London stage.

Young England was written by Walter Reynolds, a bank
official from Leeds. It was supposed to demonstrate the joys
of being a Scout, the virtues of a healthy lifestyle and the
ultimate punishment for all cads and blackguards. Unfortunately the audience refused to take it at all seriously and
treated it as though it were an uproarious comedy, learning
all the lines and joining in with the actors. The play opened
at the Victoria Palace Theatre on Monday Sept. 10, 1934 and
ran for 273 performances at a succession of West End
Theatres. It was, without doubt, the most successful bad play
ever written.

Act One is set in London 'early in the Great War'. Three
'loose women' enter – one of them a new recruit who has, to
the shock of the audience, just left the Girl Guides – it really
makes you wonder what badges she'd been taking in her
troop. They relate how they came to this sorry pass:

> MARGARET: God! Why did I ever begin? and you – Look here Lou,
> How the Hell did you, a prize scholar at the Council School,
> come to take up such a life as this?
>
> LOUISA: Oh the usual, before the war I couldn't get a job and I
> wouldn't go into service. Being idle I got bored beyond words –
> went to a night club, swallowed some rotten cocktails and cheap
> champagne –
>
> MARGARET: Fast train to hell –

It has the gritty feel of Zola, I think you'll agree. Before you can say 'teetotal' she was seduced, abandoned, began a life of crime and ended up a prostitute. I for one, will never touch a cocktail again. And, lest you think that there is no more to be told, Mr Reynolds hints at even further depravity; as Louisa exits she is followed by a Chinaman saying, 'Hi Mlissy, Mlissy, white powder!'[1] She goes offstage to try to throw herself under a bus. By now the audience are seriously considering copying her.

As well as showing us the depths of depravity awaiting any Girl Guide who strays off the true path, we are also introduced to characters such as Jabez Hawk and Ronald Spence. Jabez is a cad and a bounder who has married a woman and then abandoned her to die amidst the filth and the squalor and the Chinese laundrymen. We know he is a cad because throughout the play he wears a top hat. Ronald is an unfrocked priest who is now a photographer. We are not told why Ronald has been defrocked, but I suspect it was for over-acting.

At the end of the first Act, Jabez escapes, his girl collapses, there is an air-raid and an un-named girl dies whilst giving birth in the Salvation Army shelter. A lady called Mrs Ravenscroft decides to adopt the orphan boy.

Act Two opens twenty years later.[2] Jabez Hawk is now Mayor of Carlingford, and is still a scoundrel, although he

---

[1] I suppose he could have been doing her laundry and asking for more soap...

[2] Not literally, that would be a rather long intermission. Mind you, at least you'd have a chance of getting served at the bar.

manages to fool all the people by the crafty ruse of keeping a Bible and a copy of *The Pilgrim's Progress* open on his desk. The orphan boy has grown up to be Hope Ravenscroft, strapping young man, scout-leader, Town Councillor, engineer and prospective MP. He has also won the Bronze Cross and two life saving medals – one of which was for diving into a millstream to save the life of a socialist, which is surely an act beyond the call of duty. Hope is opposing Jabez at the forthcoming parliamentary election.

> JABEZ: *Yes and Ravenscroft knows all the tricks and above all, he'll use his Boy Scouts as a lever to lift him into the House of Commons.*

I am not sure how the Boy Scouts have this power – surely most of them would be too young to vote? Of course, there is always the possibility that Hope is drilling them into a kind of Hitler Youth... However, Jabez and his son Jabez Jr decide to get rid of Hope. Jabez Jr steals £200 from the safe at a Scout Camp that Hope is running and leaves clues framing Hope for the theft.

Indeed, the entrance to the Scout Camp is one of my favourite scenes in the play. The stage is full of life and action:

> *(General entrance)*
> *(Enter Dr Inglehurst and Mrs Ravenscroft conversing together pleasantly.)*
> *(Lady Mary runs eagerly and in great relief to Mrs Ravenscroft.)*
> *(Enter various groups of Scouts and Guides with their leaders, male and female.)*
> *(Enter Hope Ravenscroft leading a troop of Scouts. Hope bows to Lady Mary – Lady Mary betrays evident pleasure at seeing Hope.)*
> *(Jabez notices their demeanour, and scowls.)*
> *(The various contingents as they enter take up positions at the back till the stage is filled.)*
> *(Enter a boy on a penny farthing bicycle.)*
> *(Enter a girl on a modern motor cycle.)*

Why a boy is taking his penny farthing to camp is never satisfactorily explained. Perhaps he is a late arrival from Act One. After yet more entrances the scene continues with a rousing speech from our hero:

> HOPE (*always natural and unaffected – pleasantly familiar and with gay light comedy*): Well boys, we've tramped quite a long way up hill and down dale and I suppose some of us are getting a bit tired, eh?
> BOYS: Yes Sir, not arf, just a bit, etc.

As they are so obviously 'rough types', Hope underlines the rules:

> HOPE: Well then, you Scout chaps– you of the naked knees, and you Typewriter tappers[3] – The Boy Scouts, at this, our Whitsuntide camp are only separated from the Girl Guides by just one field – and we'll use that field as a neutral ground and a meeting place – so remember you ragamuffins of Rover Cubs and wolves, you've got to be on your best behaviour – Understand?
> BOYS: Aye, Aye Sir.
> HOPE: We've got everything to make us happy – Glorious weather – Bluebells for carpets and already the lovely scent of new mown hay – Smell it!

> (*All the boys and girls sniff comically together.*)

> JABEZ JR: New mown hay! Give me tobacco –
> HOPE: I wish I could tell you how proud I am to have you young-sters all around me looking so spick and span, clean and strong and healthy – you happy wholesome boys and girls seem to me to embody the very spirit of YOUNG ENGLAND –
> the young England of today and the hope of the England and the Empire of tomorrow.

A speech which more or less sums up the play. Naturally in the end the deception is revealed, Jabez and his father are

---

[3] I have no idea what this means. Unless some of the Scouts were doing their 'Secretarial' badge.

arrested in disgrace, Hope is elected, marries his sweetheart, wins a contract to build a new bridge over the Thames and is summoned to the palace to receive a knighthood. They close by singing 'Land of Hope and Glory' and 'God Save the King'.

One of the finest scenes in the piece is the fight scene between Hope and Jabez Jr. It is a masterpiece of stagecraft.

> JABEZ (rolling up his shirt sleeves): Oh – ain't you coming on? man? don't stand there shivering like a sheep – ladies like a man that shows a little pluck – and if you hold back any longer I shall have to lay you on your back – (After hopping round him he aims a blow at Hope. Hope fells Jabez, who falls flat on his back from the single blow.) [NOTE — Get Boxing expert's advice for the scrap.][4] (The Scouts let out a war yell.)

> SCOUTS: Lift him up shoulder high,
> Lift him up the winner,
> Yah, Boom, Rah – the winner,
> Lift him up, Yah, Boom Rah!
> The winner.

Proof that Walter Reynolds could also write terrible poetry when he put his mind to it.

The play also includes a Scout show – described by the author as the 'finest male and female variety performance procurable, suitable to boy and Rover Scouts and to Girl Guides and Guiders'. Details of this interlude are sketchy, but Reynolds suggests items such as a whistling solo, skating, acrobats and the Carlisle Children's band. Frankly if it included every item he suggests, it would add about another hour and a half to the performance.

As a piece of theatre, you have to admit that *Young England* has everything – songs, fight scenes, boys on penny farthings, and more bare legs than you can shake a woggle at.

[4] The request in brackets is in the book of the play. Like all great artists, Walter was not too proud to admit when he didn't know how to depict something.

It was no surprise that it became the huge hit that it was, nor that the audience should try to join in.

Unfortunately this didn't always please Walter who used to patrol the aisles, shaking his stick at the crowd. Some performances – shades of MacGonagall – had even to be cancelled because of crowd behaviour.

As one news report put it:

> *Owing to persistent interruptions from a section of the audience, the National Anthem was played and the curtain run down 20 minutes before Young England should have ended its run at Daley's on Saturday night...*

Walter Reynolds was quoted as saying

> *'From the second or third night after the production of the play a number of disorderly people, mostly students, have come to the performances and got beyond control.' Mr Reynolds added that some of the interrupters had seen the play over 100 times. They knew every line of the play and shouted the words in advance of the performers.*

It is no mystery why *Young England* was such a success. The biggest mystery is how it got put on in the first place. Did Mr Reynolds bank roll it? Was it funded as a piece of Scout propaganda? Whatever the case it ended its run on 18 May, 1935 and has never, as far as I know, been performed since.

This is a tragedy. The time is obviously ripe for a revival. Indeed, we could even stage a Walter Reynolds season, since the fly-leaf of the published edition lists another 17 undiscovered works including *A Mother's Sin*, *The Nation's Curse (The Drink Question)* and *Jack's Wedding*.

Imagine – a season at the National Theatre. Featuring Kenneth Branagh as Hope, Nicole Kidman as Lady Mary, Sir Ian McKellern as Jabez and with a special guest appearance of Jack Nicholson as 'Boy on the penny farthing'.

Bibliography

Young England, A Play in Two Periods, London, Victor
   Gollancz, 1935

☞ Four Stars and Better
Margaret Cavendish; James McIntyre; Joseph Gwyer; Julia
Moore; William MacGonagall; Francis Saltus Saltus; Theo.
Marzials; Pedro Carolino; Shepherd M. Dugger; Amanda
McKittrick Ros

☞ Plays and Verse Drama
William Nathan Stedman; James Henry Powell; Francis
Saltus Saltus

✲✲

Keith Odo Newman (fl. 1945)
Professional Audience Member

In Keith Odo Newman's masterwork, *The 250 Times I Saw A Play*, he relates, in excruciating detail, his experiences as a serial attender. Apparently as some kind of exercise in psychology, he watched the same play two hundred and fifty times, both in rehearsals and in performance, and the book follows this process and recounts his reflections on the remarkable experience.

Frustratingly for the reader, however, he neglects to tell us what the play was, who was in it, or even why he decided to do such a stupid thing in the first place.[1]

The book was published in 1945, accompanied by a 'facsimile of a comment from George Bernard Shaw' which begins helpfully 'I don't know what to say about this book.'

Shaw continues

> *The experience on which it is founded is so extraordinary, that an honest record of it should be preserved. But it would have driven me mad; and I am not sure that the author came out of it without a slight derangement.*

Understandably, Keith did not find the experience easy:

> *It was, by common agreement, and still is, an excellent play. The cast was, by equally common agreement, an excellent cast. The production too was highly praised. Yet I suffered severely and I don't complain ... Matinée or evening performance, rain or shine, found me in my seat.*

---

[1] He even claims to have thought up the title of the play in the first place, but still won't say what it was.

This man is a martyr. A stupid martyr, admittedly, but still a martyr. It was the relatively early days that he found most difficult, but soon he overcame these teething troubles:

> I learned to sleep, open-eyed, through the more irksome passages of the play, though I would not be too sure that, on occasions, I did not proffer the traditional aspect of peaceful slumber. Be that as it may, I woke, almost invariably, with a jerk when a deviation from the original script occurred. I woke therefore quite often. At times – but I may have only imagined it – I caught a stony glance from the stage. This would have been quite justified, if my observation was correct, as it must be aggravating to a degree, to any actor to be made an unwilling witness to such a hypnotic effect of his art.

Soon his attendance began to invoke an almost drug-like state of altered consciousness:

> After a comparatively short time of serial attendance I began to see everything on stage as through a magnifying-glass. All seemed to assume an undue importance.

His scrutiny was such that he even noticed when

> the actor's eye at some performances rolled in fine frenzy, instead of carrying out its usual swinging movements along a horizontal axis...

After a while, understandably, he began to get a bit critical. He had to repress the urge to shout at the actors. And he grew particularly sensitive to what he calls 'smackers' – not the physical punishment, but

> a peculiar smacking noise produced by the collaboration of lips and tongue... It's purpose is, on stage, primarily to establish confidence in the person who creates this hideous disturbance.

I think he means what we would call 'tutting', but I am not sure. Nevertheless, his analytical mind was of great help to the actors in stamping out this vile habit:

> *As I returned to the theatre in the early afternoon, she interrupted her performance* [this was during a rehearsal] *and told me, in the most amiable way, that her neighbour during lunch had informed her that I had said she had smacked nine times during sixteen minutes. I replied immediately that there must have been some mistake. The truth was that I had counted sixteen times in nine minutes.*

How they didn't smack him is beyond belief. It is not as if this continued attendance granted him any unique insight. Here is one of his deeper thoughts:

> *The longer I continued my attendances, the more did I become convinced that a play, to be fully appreciated and enjoyed, must not only be played, but played before an audience...*

In the end, he comes to believe that, in a strange way, 'all the world's a stage' and that he has been writing about the bigger picture after all. The book closes with the stirring observation

> *Often have I felt when I read about Life, that I was reading about the Stage. Now, writing about the Stage, I find that I wrote about Life after TWO HUNDRED AND FIFTY TIMES I SAW A PLAY.*

The reader, after ninety-two pages of this stuff, is drawn to the conclusion that far from writing about life, Keith Odo Newman would have done far better to go out and get one.

Bibliography

The 250 Times I Saw A Play, Oxford, Pelagos Press, 1944

☞ Philosophy and Theology
Margaret Cavendish; The Devout Salutationist; 'Lord' Timothy Dexter; Eliza Cook; William Nathan Stedman

The Five Golden Rules of Bad Writing
5. The Opposite Effect

This, of all the rules, is the golden test of a truly bad writer: the writing must have the opposite effect to that which was intended.

Whatever their purpose in writing, whatever emotion they were attempting to stir, the truly bad writer always manages to achieve exactly the opposite. They aim for the moon, but only succeed in shooting themselves in the foot.

Their tragic poems make us weep, it is true, but only with laughter. A verse in praise of the temperance movement inevitably leaves one needing a stiff drink. Passages that are designed to show us how cute children can be leave us with the overwhelming desire to beat the little brats about the head with planks.

Mournful celebrations of death do not, in the hands of a bad writer, lead the reader to contemplate their own fate, their unconscious humour and wonderful badness make you feel glad to be alive.

For example . . .
Oh, just open a page of this book at random . . .

The Greatest
of Them All

*****

Amanda McKittrick Ros (1860–1939)
The Greatest of Them All

Amanda McKittrick Ros is the greatest bad writer who ever
lived. A master – or rather mistress, for she was nothing if not
formidably female – of both poetry and prose, a gloriously
over-the-top writer who was utterly convinced of her own
greatness and of the merits of her work.

Amanda's fame rests primarily on her novels, the most difficult form of bad writing, for it is a large-scale work. It is easier to be gloriously bad in fourteen lines of verse than it is in
two hundred and fifty pages of prose – few people have the
energy, the invention, the sheer depths to write a truly bad
novel. Most bad writers are bad in patches. Amanda was bad
for long periods at a time – in fact she was bad all the time.

As Anna Margaret McKittrick, she was born in Drumaness,
near Ballynahinch, Ireland, on 8 December 1860. Her father
was a schoolteacher who tried to teach his daughters French
and German. 'I stuck to the English language chiefly,' she
wrote later, 'nor do I regret it one bit.'[1]

When she was twenty she moved to Larne to become a
teacher and it was there she married Andrew Ross, the station master. Andy Ross was a strong and determined man,
but he was nothing compared to his wife, and throughout
their marriage there was no doubt who wore the trousers.[2]
She was proud of him, however, and in later years was given
to making extravagant claims for her husband, such as claiming that he was the close friend of Randolph Churchill and,
more bafflingly, that he could speak Norwegian.

---

[1] No one has ever asked how the English language felt about her sacrifice.
[2] In a figurative sense. Amanda would *never* have actually worn trousers.

Amanda was greatly influenced by Marie Corelli[3] and in the late 1890s she began to write. Her writing immediately started to transform her. As fiction began to pour forth from her, so it began partially to take over her life. She dropped the last 's' from her husband's name – perhaps to link herself to the ancient family of de Ros in Co. Down – and in 1897, with the publication of her first book, *Irene Iddlesleigh*, 'Amanda McKittrick Ros' burst on to the literary stage.

The opening lines of *Irene Iddlesleigh* set the tone for all her later work:

> *Sympathize with me indeed! Ah, no! Cast your sympathy on the chill waves of troubled waters, fling it on the oases of futurity: dash it against the rock of gossip: or better still, allow it to remain within the false and faithless bosom of buried scorn. Such were the few remarks of Irene as she paced the beach of limited freedom, alone and unprotected.*

Irene Iddesleigh is a tale of a mismatched marriage. Irene marries Sir John Dunfern, but she is really in love with her tutor, Oscar Otwell. Sir John first gets hints of this when, before the marriage, he surprises them together in the conservatory.

> *'Can it be possible?' exclaimed Sir John in profound astonishment … Irene, rising to her feet in a second was utterly dazed, and had the dim lights shewed her proud face to an advantage, the ruddy glow of deepest crimson guilt would have manifested itself to a much greater degree. Making multitudinous apologies, etc.,[4] she at once joined Sir John who led her back, in apparent triumph, to share the next waltz.*

It does not bode well. It is clear that Irene is only marrying Sir John for the money. Suspicious thought keeps 'tickling his warm enthusiasm with the nimble fingers of jealousy'. And if you've ever had your enthusiasm tickled, you will know it is not a comfortable feeling. Marriage day looms and Amanda declares:

---

[3] Though, unlike William Stedman, she had no desire to marry the lady.

[4] This 'etc.' is unusual. In her later work, Amanda would never have truncated a piece of prose in this way. Instead we would be given the full text of the apology, possibly with some heaving of the chest thrown in as well.

Great mercy! Only another week and I shall cease to be a free-thinker.

Quite what she means is open to debate. She may be implying that Sir John can assert a kind of mind control.[5] Or she
may be considering becoming a vicar. Rejecting a white dress
– or 'the garb of glistening glory' – she turns up to the marriage wearing a dark green frock. The marriage, incidentally,
is being performed by 'the Bishop of Barelegs' and 'Canon
Foot'.

Rapidly things start to go wrong in the marriage. After
only six months, Sir John's hair has started to turn white.
Well, not white. More 'snowy':

> 'I, as you see, am tinged with slightly snowy tufts, the result of sti-
> fled sorrow and care concerning you alone; and on the memorable day
> of our alliance, as you are well aware, the black and glossy locks of
> glistening glory crowned my brow… I was enticed to believe that
> an angel was always hovering around my footsteps, when moodily
> engaged in resolving to acquaint you of my great love, and undying
> desire to place you upon the highest pinnacle possible of praise and
> purity within my power to bestow!'

'Moodily' here makes him sound like a grumpy adolescent. I
think she means 'emotionally'. Or maybe he was depressed –
maybe he was unconsciously thinking of his snowy tufts.
Whatever the case, he feels he has been tricked into a lot of
climbing.

> 'Was I duped to ascend the ladder of liberty, the hill of harmony, the
> tree of triumph, and the rock of regard, and when wildly manifesting
> my act of ascension, was I to be informed of treading still in the
> valley of defeat?'

No wonder he's turning white, he must be knackered. He
goes on to appeal to her to put him out of his misery, in one
of Amanda's most famous quotes:

---

[5] He probably learnt it from Gladstone.

'Speak! Irene! Wife! Woman! Do not sit in silence and allow the blood
that now boils in my veins to ooze through cavities of unrestrained
passion and trickle down to drench me with its crimson hue!'

Irene does not answer him. She cannot understand him.
I cannot understand him. His snowy tufts and wild manifes-
tations have driven him to the point of madness. The truth
will out, however, and nine months later, after having given
birth to a son, she falls into a fever during which she 'issues
a multitude of touchy remarks' concerning her 'darling and
much loved tutor'. Sir John, suspecting she plans to elope,
takes her to a room in the castle.

'This,' said Sir John, 'is the room of correction, the room of death. It
defies escape or secretion...'

Irene is imprisoned, but with the help of her maid she
escapes, or possibly secretes, and elopes with her true love.
However, he loses his job, and pretty soon 'Oscar was beginning to near his purse's wrinkled bottom'. They decide to
emigrate to America where they are bigamously married.
     Sir John, hearing of the marriage, calls his solicitors

and ordering his will to be produced, demanded there and then that
the pen of persuasion be dipped in the ink of revenge and spread thick-
ly along the paragraph of blood-related charity to blank the intolera-
ble words that referred to the woman he was now convinced, beyond
doubt, had braved the bridge of bigamy.

By now, the reader has walked up the avenue of astonish-
ment and arrived at the heaven of hilarity. The tale, however,
ends tragically. After years of struggle, Oscar turns to drink
and takes to inflicting 'strokes of abuse' on his wife. He
drowns himself and Irene returns to Ireland to ask forgive-
ness of Sir John. However, Sir John has died of a broken heart
and whilst visiting his grave, Irene has an uncomfortable
encounter with her son Sir Hugh, now Lord Dunfern:

'Mighty heaven!' exclaimed Sir Hugh Dunfern, 'are you the vagrant
who ruined the very existence of him whom you now profess to have

> loved? You, the wretch of wicked and wilful treachery, and formerly
> the wife of him before whose bones you falsely kneel! ... False woman!
> Wicked wife! Detested mother! Bereft widow!'

(It's not going well then...)

> 'Ah, woman of sin and stray companion of tutorism, arise, I demand
> you, and strike across that grassy centre as quickly as you can,
> and never more make your hated face appear within these mighty
> walls.'

And so, this destitute 'companion of tutorism' flees and, alas,
dies. The novel ends with a lesson we would all do well to
learn:

> Life is too often stripped of its pleasantness by the steps of false
> assumption, marring the true path of life-long happiness, which
> should be pebbled with principle, piety, purity and peace.

Irene Iddlesleigh is one of the great novels. It is right up there
with Tolstoy's *War and Peace*, Dickens's *Bleak House* and *The
Balsam Groves of Grandfather Mountain* by Shepherd M. Dugger.
On initial publication – paid for by her husband as an
anniversary present – *Irene Iddlesleigh* garnered little attention. But then it was taken up by Barry Pain, a critic and
humorist, in a review called 'The Book of the Century'.
Instantly, Amanda was a celebrity – although she never forgave Pain for his mockery, and from that moment regarded
critics as her sworn enemies.

Indeed, her second great work, *Delina Delaney*, begins with
a long essay entitled 'Criticism of Barry Pain against *Irene
Iddlesleigh*' in which the critic is torn to shreds in inimitable
Amanda style:

> This so-called Barry Pain, by name, has taken upon him to criticize
> a work the depth of which fails to reach the solving power of his
> borrowed, and, he'd have you believe, varied talent.

But this is mild stuff. No doubt, as it preceded her novel,
Amanda felt she had to hold herself back. Elsewhere she

scourges critics – not just Barry Pain but others such as D.B. Wyndham Lewis (whom she christened St Scandalbags) and worst of all, the American Thomas Beer, whom she never forgave for saying that she was 'wife to a workman'. Over the years she was to turn her considerable talent for vitriol and abuse on these critics, calling them 'Bastard Donkey-headed Mites', 'Denouncing Arabs' 'Drunken Ignorant Dross', 'Rodents of State' and 'Maggoty Numskulls' among many other names.

In *Delina Delaney* her style has matured, grown ... mutated. It begins with possibly the most baffling opening sentence in literature:

> *Have you ever visited that portion of Erin's plot that offers its sympathetic soil for the minute survey and scrutinous examination of those in political power, whose decision has wisely been the means before now of converting the stern and prejudiced, and reaching the hand of slight aid to share its strength in augmenting its agricultural richness?*

I first read this sentence nearly three years ago. Since then, I have read it once a week in an increasingly desperate search for meaning. But I still don't understand it. It is magnificent in its impenetrable mystery; it is the riddle of the sphinx, the smile of the Mona Lisa. It sounds wonderful, but remains impervious to comprehension. I know it has something to do with the western borders of Ireland, for that is where *Delina Delaney* starts, but beyond that I cannot say why the soil is being examined and who is looking at it.

It is a fine example of the difference between *Delina Delaney* and *Irene Iddlesleigh*. *Delina* is a more complex work – nearly twice as long as *Irene* and rich with wonderful phrases. In *Irene Iddlesleigh* there are only twelve speeches and none of the minor characters says anything; in *Delina* you cannot shut anyone up. Even on their death bed they still manage a good four pages of eloquent drivel.

Delina also shows perfectly Amanda's unique use of language. For Amanda, eyes are 'piercing orbs', legs are 'bony supports'; people do not blush, they are 'touched by the hot hand of bewilderment'.[6]

Delina, like *Irene*, has more than its fair share of death and disaster. Delina's father dies rescuing people from a shipwreck, whilst Lord Gifford's mother goes mad when she finds out he is engaged to a seamstress. She is told of this by Lady Mattie Maynard, a rejected fiancée of Lord Gifford's, and expresses her madness in the usual Ros style:

> *'Henry Edward Ludlow Gifford, son of my strength, idolized remnant of my inert husband, who at this moment invisibly offers the scourging whip of fatherly authority to your backbone of resentment…'*

She begins to pray, addressing God as 'Pater'. Truly this woman is an aristocrat.

> *'Heavenly Pater,' she began, 'listen to the words of a daughter of affliction, and chase, I pray Thee, instantly, the dismal perplexities that presently clog the filmy pores of her weary brain into the stream of trickling nothingness. Bind their origin with cloth of coloured shame, and restore, Thou, her equilibrium with draughts of soothing good.'*

It has to be said that none of the characters in *Irene* have much depth. Sir John is not what you might call a rounded character, although his habit of locking his wives in a disused dungeon might be said to be eccentric, but in *Delina* the characters live.

The finest character in the book is the scheming governess, Madame-de-Maine. She joins the household when Lord Gifford and Delina move to London, causes Delina to run away and turns Lord Gifford into an alcoholic by dosing him with brandy. She even shoots the old servant, Joss, when he finds out the truth, and such is her coolness, she sings a song over the body.

---

[6] My own favourite phrase comes from St Scandalbags – one of her diatribes against a critic, where she refers to trousers as 'southern necessities'.

Delina eventually returns and, for a moment, it looks as though Madame-de-Maine's schemes are to be foiled. But she is made of sterner stuff and she frames Delina for the attempted murder of Lord Gifford, by hiding a poisoned pudding in the girl's room. Delina is put on trial and sentenced to five years' penal servitude, causing uproar in the court:

> *A panic swept over the entire court, whilst Delina fell heavily against the front of the dock.*
> *Lord Gifford groaned aloud.*
> *A laugh of devilish triumph lit up the features of Madame-de-Maine. Ladies became hysterical, some fainting, others weeping copiously, and nothing was heard save sobbing and wailing. One girl named Fanny Fowler, who had been a companion of Delina's at school, died from the shock...*

The judge, it has to be said, is worryingly imprecise in his summing up:

> *'Delina Delaney, you have been found guilty of this horrible crime by a jury of your own countrymen... You were set apart to attend to the wants of Lord Gifford and devote your untiring energy to his comfort. Being tempted through some motive or other to administer to him certain deadly poisons you must now suffer the consequences.'*

Delina goes to prison, but it soon becomes clear that, devilish triumph or not, Madame-de-Maine has not succeeded. She rushes to Lord Gifford's side only to be told:

> *'Begone from my presence, you wicked woman, servant of the devil, your daily advocate. Begone sister of sin and mother of malice! Conspiring demon! Dare to offer your bony extremity to me or your milky words that sound as so many shots from the mouth of a machine gun!'*

She, and her bony extremities, flee to America where, some time later, after descending into a haze of drink and gambling, she dies. On her death bed she confesses the truth to Lord Gifford, who just happened to be in the neighbourhood. In the end Delina marries Lord Gifford and all ends happily, but not before a final, dramatic twist. Here I am faced with a difficulty, for this is the most ludicrous plot twist in the history of literature. It demands to be shared with all lovers of the truly ludicrous, yet I am loath to give it away. So if you really must know, consult the appendix at the back of this book. Otherwise, get hold of a copy of *Delina Delaney* and read it for yourself.

Delina Delaney and *Irene Iddlesleigh* were the only two novels that Amanda published in her lifetime. A forgotten manuscript, *Helen Huddleson*, was published in 1969, but it is more experimental. The villains, for example, are all named after fruit, starting with the gloriously named Lord Raspberry, continuing with his sister Cherry Raspberry, and including Sir Peter Plum, Mrs Greengage and Sir Christopher Currant. The only vegetable is a maid called Lily Lentil.

Quite why Amanda decided on this approach is uncertain, but it certainly adds to the interest. Also, much of the book is written in an impenetrable dialect which, when Jack Loudan came to edit the book, had literally to be translated. Here is a brief example:

> *...an' furbye dthe folk says haes a nothing' ive a buddy til luck at, an' is lack Lewis (anodther windy yapp dthat snarls and barks) ... haes owl fadther was a labourin'-man...*[7]

Nevertheless, the book contains some fine examples of her writing. I am particularly fond of the passage where Lord Raspberry proposes to her:

> *He looked upon her where she stood gasping, her bleached lips quivering, her hand upon the weapon she still regarded with awe. He gave her a murderous stare, exclaiming in frenzy:*
>
> *'Helen, Helen, 'tis all your fault. I'll give you another minute to decide...'*

[7] It roughly translates as '...and another thing, the folk say he's a nothing of a body to look at, and is like Lewis (another windy yapp that snarls and barks) ... his old father was a labouring-man ...' Yes, she is talking about Thomas Beer and Wyndham Lewis again.

He counts the seconds and, just when the reader can bear it no longer, she gives in:

> *He counted the seconds and on reaching fifty-nine she clasped him in her trembling arms – shouting:*
>
> *'I will – I will marry you, Lord Raspberry.'*
>
> *She then fell fainting at his feet. He placed the little figure on a couch, ran for some brandy and raising her gently applied the stimulant. Soon, however, she rallied – screaming – shouting – laughing – weeping alternatively.*

This hardly seems like 'rallying' to me, and one feels she is not entirely happy with the engagement. *Helen Huddleson* is an interesting book – one can see Amanda trying new ideas, like the dialect characters and the story within a story. Sadly, she died before it could be completed. The version that finally made it into print was completed by her biographer, Jack Loudan.[8]

If Amanda had written just those novels, her immortality would be assured. But, to the joy of bad verse fans everywhere, she was also a poet, publishing two books of poetry during her lifetime, *Poems of Puncture* (1912) and *Fumes of Formation* (1933).

Poems of Puncture was published, she admitted, as 'an act of revenge'. She was engaged at the time in a number of legal disputes – particularly over the fate of a lime-kiln which she had inherited and was forced to sell. Much of *Poems of Puncture* is therefore dedicated to abusing lawyers or the

---

[8] There was one further fragment of a novel, published in 1954 as *Donald Dudley, The Bastard Critic*. It is a slightly unhinged book, which depicts in a style reminiscent of Zola the squalid life of your average literary critic. Donald, who is painfully aware of the treachery and base indecency of his calling, lives in a rat-infested slum with a landlady who belongs to 'that class who subsist on the prostitute penny'. He augments his income by chopping wood, mending boots and, apparently, 'loitering adjacent to the General Post Office'. The small fragment we have of this work appears to indicate that it was to be a Faustian tale, whereby Donald makes a pact with a mysterious gentleman called Mr Devildinger who eyes the critic 'with his greenish orbs'.

many people with whom she had had legal disputes. Her most famous poem from this collection begins:

> Readers, did you ever hear
> Of Mickey Monkeyface McBlear?

And after that it gets quite rude. In truth, the poems are too vitriolic to be much fun.

During World War I, writing under an assumed name,[9] she published a series of patriotic poems which were sold for various good causes. The best of these is 'A Little Belgian Orphan', which tells of the awful suffering of one small boy in occupied Belgium.

> Daddy was a Belgian and so was Mammie too,
> And why I'm now in Larne I want to tell you;
> Daddy was a soldier and fought his level best...

However, while Daddy is at the front, the Germans sneak round the back, as it were, and enter the cosy family home:

> One spoke to Mammie, saying – 'Stay your labour for your kids,
> Give to us all this bread, or we'll stab your bony ribs.'
> And raising high his glittering sword cut off poor Mammie's head,
> Her body fell upon me while her poor neck bled and bled.

After this things turn nasty:

> Just then they raised the little lad and threw him on the fire
> And wreathed in smiles they watched him burn until he did expire...

The poem ends with a wonderfully patriotic exhortation to the troops:

> Go! Meet the foe undaunted, they're rotten cowards all,
> Present to them the bayonet, they totter and they fall,
> We know you'll do your duty and come to little harm
> And if you meet the Kaiser, cut off his other arm.

---

[9] 'Monica Moyland'. The alliteration probably gave it away, but at least she didn't call herself after a fruit.

To be fair to Amanda, this kind of propaganda was only what the majority of the populace believed at the time, it's just that most of the populace didn't write bad poetry.

Fumes of Formation, her final volume of poetry, is a marvellously rich collection. The title page tells us that

> *This inventive production was hatched within a mind fringed with Fumes of Formation, the Ingenious Innings of Inspiration and Thorny Tincture of Thought.*

Just in case you thought she simply knocked the things out. Her poem 'Eastertide' boasts one of the great opening lines of bad poetry:

> *Dear Lord the day of eggs is here*

Whilst the rather over-titled 'On visiting Westminster Abbey a "reduced dignity" invited me to muse on its merits' begins

> *Holy Moses! Have a look!*
> *Flesh decayed in every nook!*

Several of the poems rail against the indecencies of modern life. 'Days of Decency – Dead!' runs

> *Dead centuries showed the body clad*
> *   Of girl or lad;*
> *This century exposes all*
> *   Both large and small…*

And in 'The Old Home' she indicates how surprisingly revealing the modern garments are:

> *The petticoat faded away as we do*
> *In circumference it covered not one leg but two,*
> *Its successor exposes the arms, breasts and necks,*
> *Legs, knees and thighs and too often – the –*

She declines to give the last word and, true to her spirit, I leave you to work it out for yourself. All I can say is that clothing in Ireland must have been cut very short.

The poems in *Fumes of Formation* are generally free from the kind of vitriol that marred *Poems of Puncture*, but there are a couple of poems on her enemies, including the poem called 'The End of "Pain"' which celebrates the death of her nemesis, Barry.

> That 'Pain' has ceased to mock, to mar
> Those gems he picked up near and far,
> Is evident. His pricky pen
> Reclaim it ne'er shall he again.
> A mighty maggot, he thought he,
> A slavey now to Master D.

The syntax is somewhat confused but 'Master D.' is obviously the devil and the phrase 'he thought he' strikes a certain reggae note. One can imagine Bob Marley singing it.[10]

Another poem, 'Epitaph', concludes rather ungraciously

> Of virtue little, 'twas her fate
> To part with it when out of date
> Her name was 'Tulip,' I declare
> To give her other name – Don't care.

Amanda was never short of enemies to write about. A devout puritan, she was capable of crude language, vitriolic behaviour and enormous arrogance. Yet there is a kind of innocence about her as well, because she never realizes how ludicrous she is being. Her visiting card ran 'Mrs Amanda M. Ros, Authoress – At Home Always to the Honourable.'

Even in death she could be unforgiving. When her husband died she didn't approve of some of the mourners who turned up, so told the hearse to move off at a trot. The mourners were left with the choice of either running behind the carriage or going home. She even sent some of their

---

[10] Although no doubt he would have struggled with the next lines, which run

> He in his glassless backroom bare
> Can flaunt his sheets of 'blarney' there…

wreaths back, employing a man to go round the town with a wheelbarrow delivering the rejected offerings.[11]

But without that pride, would she have written as she did? Would she have created these wonderfully wrong-headed, over-written books?

'My chief object in writing is and always has been to write if possible in a strain all my own,' she once wrote. 'My works are all expressly my own – pleasingly peculiar – not a borrowed stroke in one of them.'

How true. No one has ever written like Amanda McKittrick Ros. No one else ever will.

Bibliography

Irene Iddesleigh, Belfast, 1897 (reprinted by the Nonesuch Press in 1926 and in the US by Boni & Liveright in 1927)

Delina Delaney, Belfast, 1898 (reprinted by Chatto & Windus in 1935)

Poems of Puncture, London, 1912

Fumes of Formation, Belfast, 1933

Donald Dudley, the Bastard Critic, Thames Ditton, 1954

Helen Huddleson, London, 1969

☞ Death, Disaster and Disease
Julia Moore; William MacGonagall; Eliza Cook; James Henry Powell; The *Titanic* Poets

☞ Dialects and Accents
J. Stanyan Bigg; James Whitcomb Riley; 'Child' Poems

---

[11] In 1922 she married again, to a farmer from the wonderfully named Clintnagooland, Co. Down. He was comparatively wealthy, allowing Amanda to concentrate on her writing for the rest of her life.

☞ Four Stars and Better

Margaret Cavendish; James McIntyre; Joseph Gwyer; Julia
Moore; William MacGonagall; Francis Saltus Saltus;
Théophile Marzials; Pedro Carolino; Walter Reynolds;
Shepherd M. Dugger

☞ Made-Up Words and Strange Syntax

'Lord' Timothy Dexter; Leopold John Manners De Michele;
Théophile Marzials; Pedro Carolino; Nancy Luce

☞ Novels and Fiction

Margaret Cavendish; Nikolai Chernyshevsky; Shepherd M.
Dugger

Appendices

Appendix 1
Bad Writing – A Style Guide

By now, I can imagine that many of my readers are itching to get their teeth into some bad writing of their own. Here I have put together a list of recommended practices which, if used diligently, will transform any piece of writing into something memorably awful.

Body Parts

Eyes – should always be 'orbs' or, in extreme cases, 'orbicular instruments'. They can be flashing, darting or moving about in any other similar manner. If filled with tears, they should be 'lachrymal lakes' or 'gushing fountains'.

Thighs – probably best left alone, but if they must be mentioned they should be dictatorial.

Lips – use 'ruby', rather than red. 'Elastic rubies' is suitably obscure.

Legs – there is nothing poetic about legs. Use 'southernmost extremities'.

Bosoms – the opportunities are endless. Just try not to get obsessed.

Hair – should be 'raven', 'ebon', 'yellow'. It should always 'downward stream', ideally in 'sequin-studded tresses'.

Nose – use 'nasal proboscis' instead.

Noises

Bells – suggested sounds are 'dong', 'bong' or occasionally 'ting'. Extended chimes may be rendered D-O-N-G if absolutely necessary.

Machines – may be imitated by arranging the words 'thud',
'cranch', 'crunch', 'rud', 'dubber dub' and 'rub' into any
order.

Pigeons – go 'Hyüeèps' but you'll have to take my word
for it.

Sex

Sex is too mystical/poetical/messy to be referred to in a
straightforward way. Most bad writers prefer to avoid the
subject altogether. However, if you must talk about it, use
euphemistic terms such as 'my pony she tenderly patted', or
'the shadow glinted off Yani's minaret'.

Fondling is allowed, provided it is done woundlingly, or,
at a pinch, minglingly.

Bosoms may heave, throb, gleam or burst into flowering
rhododendrons.

Plants can be used symbolically, notably rhododendrons
and fennel.

Children

Children in bad writing should either be:

a   Cute, curly haired, angelic and speak 'a wickle bit wike
dis'
b   Crippled, emaciated and the offspring of drunken parents
c   Dead. Preferably run over by a train, although some
lingering wasting disease is allowed.

Autobiography

Where you are writing about yourself try to include as much
detail as possible. Remember the reader is fascinated by
everything that happens in your life, down to the minutest
detail. (The same goes for stage directions.)

Critics

These should be ignored where possible. If you must refer to them, careful use of one of the following terms is permitted: 'maggoty numskulls', 'Bastard Donkey-headed Mites', 'Denouncing Arabs', 'Drunken Ignorant Dross', or 'Rodents of State'. However, most writers choose to rise above their detractors, remembering that the more you are criticized, the greater your genius must be.

Appendix 2

Star Ratings: The World's Worst Writers in order of Merit

Five Stars

Amanda McKittrick Ros

Four Stars

Pedro Carolino
Margaret Cavendish, Duchess of Newcastle
Shepherd M. Dugger
Joseph Gwyer
William MacGonagall
James McIntyre
Théophile Marzials
Julia Moore
Walter Reynolds
Francis Saltus Saltus

Three Stars

Thomas Baker
Solyman Brown
J. Gordon Coogler
Reverend William Cook
Leopold John Manners De Michele
'The Devout Salutationist'
Edward Edwin Foot
James Grainger
Nancy Luce
William Nathan Stedman
Sir Thomas Urquhart
Reverend Samuel Wesley

Two Stars

Alfred Austin
J. Stanyan Bigg
Nikolai Chernyshevsky
Thomas Costley
Bloodgood H. Cutter
Reverend Edward Dalton
'Lord' Timothy Dexter and Jonathan Plummer
Keith Odo Newman
James Henry Powell
The *Titanic* Poets
Reverend Cornelius Whur

One Star

Eliza Cook
Stephen Fawcett
Frederick James Johnston-Smith
James Whitcomb Riley
J.B. Smiley
Pownoll Toker Williams
George Wither

Appendix 3
The Strange Ending of *Delina Delaney*

On her death bed, Madame-de-Maine not only confesses to her crime, she also reveals her true identity. At first, Lord Gifford refuses to believe it, but a simple check proves that she was speaking the truth. He asks the orderly to uncover her feet and exclaims:

> 'O God, it is true! This is my cousin, Lady Mattie Maynard! She had six toes on her right foot!'

Mattie had not entered a convent as was claimed at the end of chapter ten. She had met Madame-de-Maine and, realizing that they looked strikingly similar, murdered the French-woman and taken her place, eventually becoming Delina's guardian and governess.

Whilst this explains Madame-de-Maine's attraction to Lord Gifford, it raises a great many other issues. Primarily, of course, the question has to be asked, why didn't Lord Gifford recognize her? Mattie is described as

> '…almost a six footer, with her treadles thrust into shoes you'd swear once long ago belonged to a Chinese madman; her long, thin, wallopy legs enveloped in silken hose … her long, yellow hands, thin beyond detail, she mostly keeps powdered and jewelled with rings of every shape and form. Then her features! … Enough, – enough. But, Lord, how sharp!'

You really wouldn't have thought someone like that would be forgotten in a hurry. Somehow we have to believe either that she was a master of disguise, or that there were in the world two long-legged, six-foot-tall ladies with sharp features and yellow hands wandering about.

It gets even more complicated, for in chapter twenty-seven, she flees to America and assumes the name of Florence Fontaine. At a society ball she encounters the husband of the real Madame-de-Maine who had divorced her many years before. He is so shocked by the apparent appearance of his ex-wife that he keels over with the shock.

Unfortunately he dies before he can explain what has happened, or, as Amanda puts it, he is 'snapped from the jaws of explanation'.

I can't help wondering how many toes the real Madame-de-Maine had.

Acknowledgements

Naturally I am indebted to many of those who have gone before me.

The starting point for any study of bad writing is *The Stuffed Owl*, edited by D.B. Wyndham-Lewis and Charles Lee (London, 1930; enlarged edition, 1935). This was the first ground-breaking study of bad poetry, bringing to the attention of the world major talents such as Thomas Baker, Margaret Cavendish and James Grainger. *The Worst English Poets*, edited by Christopher Adams (London, 1958), led me on to such minor luminaries as Dalton and Costley, as well as to the magnificent Leopold John Manners De Michele. *O Rare Amanda! The Life of Amanda McKittrick Ros* by Jack Loudan (London, 1958) was invaluable, not only for his portrait of Amanda, but also for pointing me in the direction of Joseph Gwyer, Walter Reynolds and some others.

The main source for American works is *Queer Books*, by Edmund Pearson (London, 1929), which includes good stuff on Julia Moore, William Cook and Shepherd M. Dugger. There is also an excellent anthology called *Very Bad Poetry*, edited by Kathryn and Ross Petras (New York, 1997).

The most recent work on poetry alone was Nicholas T. Parsons' book *The Joy of Bad Verse* (London, 1988), a comprehensive and detailed study of virtually all the major figures.

I must also record my appreciation to Bill Thompson, who pointed me in the direction of Nikolai Chernyshevsky.

'The Poet and his Wanton Wit' by Théophile Marzials appears by kind permission of the London Library. Their kindness means the world's worst erotic poem has been saved for posterity.

Indeed, I am very grateful to the staff of several libraries – especially the London Library, the British Museum Library and the Bodleian Library, the Rhodes House Library and the Toronto Public Library – not only for their help and advice, but for not throwing me out when the giggling got too loud.

Index

A

B

E

F

G

If you have any suggestions or nominations for the World's Worst Writers, then why not visit the website?

www.worldsworstwriters.co.uk

See the portrait gallery, check out the links, find out more about the greats and leave your own nominations.

Also available from
HarperCollins*Publishers* by Nick Page

The Tabloid Shakespeare

Here are Shakespeare's plays as you've never seen them before, with hundreds of quotable lines, tragic scenes and tender poetry given the unique tabloid touch.

Inside your ballistic Bard:

'WHAT DOES HE WANT OUR EARS FOR?'
Mark Antony in plastic surgery appeal to crowd

A PAIN IN THE ASP
Cleo gets something toxic down her toga

TEENAGERS IN TERRIBLE TOMB TRAGEDY
Elopement stunt goes wrong for Romeo and Juliet

LEAR TODAY, GONERIL TOMORROW
Krazy King Karves Up His Kingdom

WHAT'S BLACK AND WHITE AND GREEN ALL OVER?
Bard Pictorial: Othello and Desdemona – the jealousy, the lust, the hankies

Plus – your guide to Shakespeare's least funny clowns, horoscopes from Macbeth's witches and cookery tips from Titus Andronicus.

The Tabloid Bible

How would the press of its day have covered the greatest story ever told? Read all about it in *The Scroll* – the only paper that was there.

Inside your supersonic *Scroll:*

WOULD YOU ADAM AND EVE IT!
Scandal as couple evicted from garden

ARKING MAD!
Nutty Noah builds the world's biggest boat in his garden. 'I'm sure he doesn't have planning permission,' says irate neighbour.

TOWER OF BABEL COLLAPSES
'Xxyshhibbothuth mi varg,' says suddenly incomprehensible builder.

ATISHOO! ATISHOO! WALL FALL DOWN!
Insurers refuse payouts over Jericho wall collapse. 'Aggressive trumpet playing is not covered,' they say.

5,000 FED WITH LOAVES AND FISHES
Miracle? Or just very thinly sliced? You decide!

Keep It Simple
(and get more out of life)

This book is for anyone who wants a less complicated life. It will help you to:

- deal with money
- simplify your possessions
- recognize your own priorities
- budget your time
- find space for quietness
- shape your own rule of life

If you want to live more simply, if you want to create space for what is really important in your life, then this friendly, funny and thought-provoking book is for you.